The Showgirl Next Door

The Showgirl Next Door

Holly Madison's Las Vegas

with photography by Denise Truscello

Editor: Heidi Knapp Rinella
Cover & Book Designer: Sue Campbell
Publishing Coordinator: Stacey Fott

ORDERING INFORMATION
Quantity sales: Special discounts are available on quantity purchases by
corporations, associations, and others. For details, contact Stephens Press.
Individual Sales: Stephens Press publications are available through most
bookstores. They can also be ordered directly from Stephens Press: (888-
951-2665); www.stephenspress.com.
Orders by book retailers and wholesalers: Stephens Press books are available
from major book wholesalers including Ingram and Baker & Taylor.

Library of Congress Cataloging-in-Publication data
Madison, Holly.
   The showgirl next door : Holly Madison's Las Vegas / Holly Madison ; Heidi
Knapp Rinella, editor.
   196 p. : photos ; 25.4 cm.

ISBN: 1-935043-31-5 (Hardcover)
ISBN-13: 978-1-935043-31-7 (Hardcover)
ISBN: 1-935043-46-3 (Trade paper)
ISBN-13: 978-1-935043-46-1 (Trade Paper)

Contents: Viva Las Vegas – Road trippin' – Las Vegas history – Suite dreams
– Holly's World – Restaurants – Vegas Vixens: the evolution of the showgirl
– Glitter Gulch – Desert Beauty – Fun Vegas Style – A peek at Peepshow –
Where in Vegas?.
   Holly Madison, former Playboy bunny and now entertainer, presents her
unique take on Las Vegas and her favorite activities and sights to see.

1. Las Vegas (Nev.)—Description and travel. I. Title.

917.93'13'5 dc22   2011   2010938540

STEPHENS PRESS, LLC
A Stephens Media Company

P.O. Box 1600 (89125-1600)
1111 West Bonanza Road
Las Vegas, Nevada 89106
(702) 386-5260
www.stephenspress.com

Printed in the Hong Kong

Dedication

**To my favorite Vegas character,
Mayor Oscar Goodman**

Holly Madison

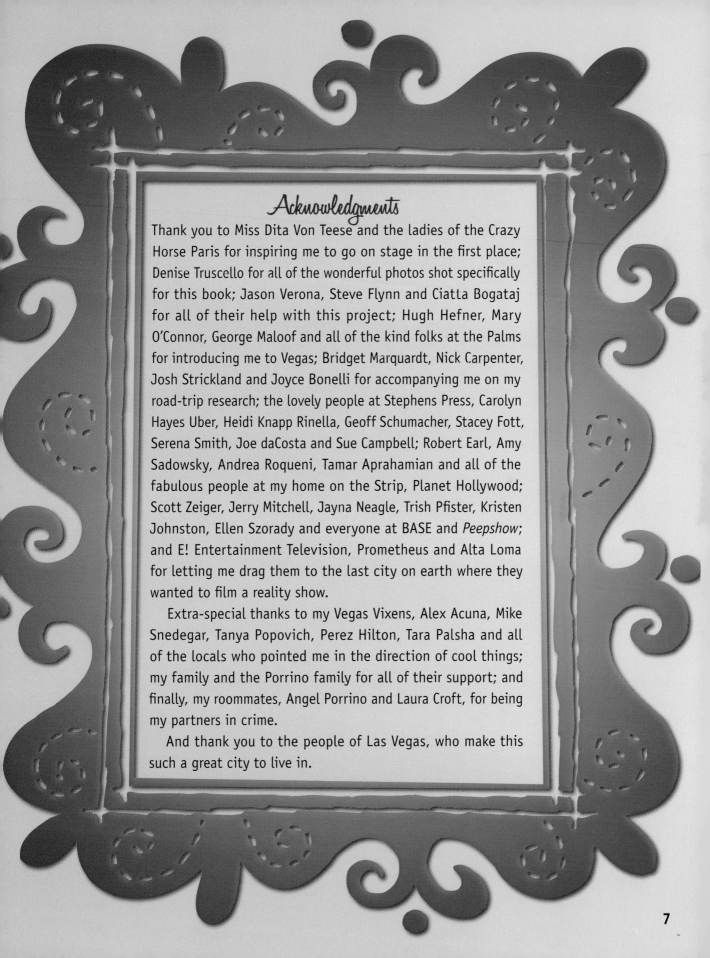

Acknowledgments

Thank you to Miss Dita Von Teese and the ladies of the Crazy Horse Paris for inspiring me to go on stage in the first place; Denise Truscello for all of the wonderful photos shot specifically for this book; Jason Verona, Steve Flynn and Ciatla Bogataj for all of their help with this project; Hugh Hefner, Mary O'Connor, George Maloof and all of the kind folks at the Palms for introducing me to Vegas; Bridget Marquardt, Nick Carpenter, Josh Strickland and Joyce Bonelli for accompanying me on my road-trip research; the lovely people at Stephens Press, Carolyn Hayes Uber, Heidi Knapp Rinella, Geoff Schumacher, Stacey Fott, Serena Smith, Joe daCosta and Sue Campbell; Robert Earl, Amy Sadowsky, Andrea Roqueni, Tamar Aprahamian and all of the fabulous people at my home on the Strip, Planet Hollywood; Scott Zeiger, Jerry Mitchell, Jayna Neagle, Trish Pfister, Kristen Johnston, Ellen Szorady and everyone at BASE and *Peepshow*; and E! Entertainment Television, Prometheus and Alta Loma for letting me drag them to the last city on earth where they wanted to film a reality show.

Extra-special thanks to my Vegas Vixens, Alex Acuna, Mike Snedegar, Tanya Popovich, Perez Hilton, Tara Palsha and all of the locals who pointed me in the direction of cool things; my family and the Porrino family for all of their support; and finally, my roommates, Angel Porrino and Laura Croft, for being my partners in crime.

And thank you to the people of Las Vegas, who make this such a great city to live in.

Contents

Viva Las Vegas!

I still remember my first trip to Vegas, when I was twenty-one. I went for a friend's birthday. She was a Playmate and I had recently moved into The Playboy Mansion, so we were going in style with Hef and a bunch of girls.

It wasn't exactly how I had pictured my first trip to Vegas, which I had assumed would be a cheap, drunken *Fear-and-Loathing*-type mess with friends who wanted to explore all of the casinos and bars. Staying at the exclusive MGM Mansions, traveling in limos like high rollers and having a packed itinerary — including all of the hottest restaurants, shows and clubs — wasn't exactly what I had expected, but hey, I'd take it!

Oh, and did I mention we arrived via private jet? There was to be no glimpse of the slot machines and blue-and-pink-patterned carpets of the McCarran International Airport terminal that time around. With my nose pressed against the glass of the limo's windows, I tried to take in as much of the Strip's skyline as I could. This was in 2001, and I remember seeing the MGM Grand's residential towers, which were still under construction. There was a sign advertising residential space for sale, and I remember thinking: "Who in the hell would want to live in Vegas? Old, retired people?" Little did I know

I would end up adopting the city as my hometown and become one of its biggest cheerleaders.

As we pulled into the MGM Mansions, I noticed we were no longer outside as such, but under a glass dome that kept the courtyard of the Tuscan-style high-roller suites impervious to weather. Not that it rains often in Vegas. I guess they had to watch out for the three days or so a year that it does.

The Mansions are the most exclusive place to stay in Vegas — so exclusive that MGM Resorts International wouldn't even give me a photo of them for this book! The Mansions are so well hidden that even though my Strip residence is right across the street, high above in Planet Hollywood, I can't see them. I have been all over the MGM Grand, through the main entryways, in and out of VIP entrances and through the property in my car as a shortcut to Planet Hollywood. Every time I craned my neck, trying to figure out where the Mansions are, and I have never seen them. They should have a name that's the opposite of The Mirage (which is down the street) because I know they are there; I just can't see them.

Anyway, back when I was rolling with someone with real star power, I actually could see the Mansions, and boy, was I impressed! Not only was the suite the size of a house, there was a swimming pool inside it! Not just a hot tub, but a whole swimming pool! Needless to say, I had never seen anything like that before.

My first impression of Vegas was that it was not what you did there; it was what was going on while you were doing it that really made the impression. For example, we went to see The *Blue Man Group* while we were there. I remember nothing about the show except getting covered in toilet paper. I also remember that the girl next to me was so drunk she spilled her strawberry daiquiri all over herself. I also remember another girl with us got pulled up on stage. And I remember going backstage to take a photo with

the Blue Men, but there were so many Playmates in the picture, I don't think I could even see myself when I got the print.

The show was in the Luxor's theater back then. As an indication of how everything in Vegas is constantly changing — or at least getting a makeover — it took me several viewings of the Cirque du Soleil show that was later performed in the same theater to remember that I had been there before.

During that first Vegas visit we had dinner at VooDoo Steak & Lounge at the Rio. I don't remember what I ate, except that it was good. Pretty much all of the food in Vegas is good, especially these days. I list my favorites later in this book, but almost every resort has an awesome steakhouse, a yummy sushi place, and a place with gourmet junk food.

What I remember about the VooDoo were the

extra Vegas-y touches that made it more than just a good meal. The cocktail menu was huge and filled with exotic drinks, some containing dry ice for a witch's-brew effect. Being at the top of the Rio, the restaurant has an amazing view of the city lights. As we stepped out on the observation deck to check out the view, one of the members of our predominantly blonde party asked, "I wonder why there haven't been any songs written about Vegas?"

"Uh . . . 'Viva Las Vegas'?" I suggested.

"Oh, yeah," was the response. No one else seemed to notice. We were here to drink, not to know what was going on — or had gone on.

Which is exactly how

Vegas likes it. With the rare exception of a few treasures like the Neon Museum, Vegas tends to tear everything down and turn implosion into spectacle in a race to make more money faster. This brings us great things we enjoy today, but we lose a lot of great stuff, too. Those nostalgic for the Rat Pack might wish they could still visit the Sands. Elvis fans might wish they could get married where Elvis and Priscilla did, in the same old Aladdin hotel. Me? I just wish the Wet 'n Wild water park were still on the Strip! There's not even anything there now, just an empty lot next to a resort site where construction has been stopped, a reflection of the bad economy of the past few years.

The beauty of Vegas, though, is that it always has an ingenious, ambitious new idea around every corner. Things are one way as I type this on my laptop in the Vegas suburbs, but by the time you have this book in your hands, who knows? Perhaps there will be a water park again.

In the seven years following my first visit, I would visit Vegas semi-regularly. It is only a fifty-minute flight from Los Angeles, where I lived for ten years, so it was super-convenient and always lots of fun. When you live in L.A., it seems like everyone you know is always going to Vegas. For many years I would stay at The Palms because of the Playboy connection (they have a Playboy Club and suite there). I still love going there because it almost feels like I

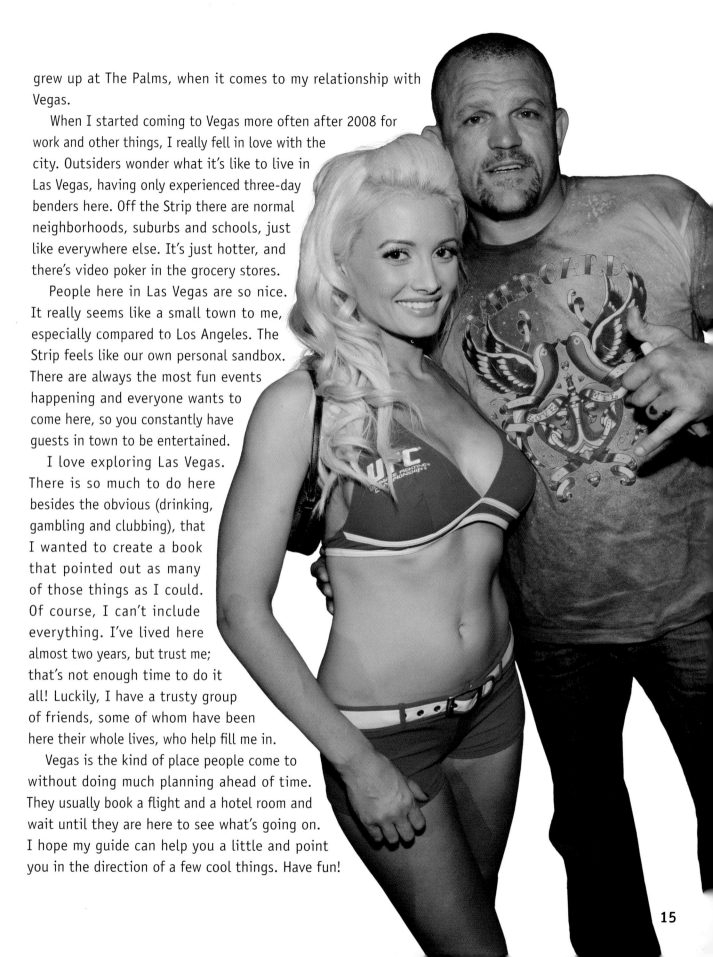

grew up at The Palms, when it comes to my relationship with Vegas.

When I started coming to Vegas more often after 2008 for work and other things, I really fell in love with the city. Outsiders wonder what it's like to live in Las Vegas, having only experienced three-day benders here. Off the Strip there are normal neighborhoods, suburbs and schools, just like everywhere else. It's just hotter, and there's video poker in the grocery stores.

People here in Las Vegas are so nice. It really seems like a small town to me, especially compared to Los Angeles. The Strip feels like our own personal sandbox. There are always the most fun events happening and everyone wants to come here, so you constantly have guests in town to be entertained.

I love exploring Las Vegas. There is so much to do here besides the obvious (drinking, gambling and clubbing), that I wanted to create a book that pointed out as many of those things as I could. Of course, I can't include everything. I've lived here almost two years, but trust me; that's not enough time to do it all! Luckily, I have a trusty group of friends, some of whom have been here their whole lives, who help fill me in.

Vegas is the kind of place people come to without doing much planning ahead of time. They usually book a flight and a hotel room and wait until they are here to see what's going on. I hope my guide can help you a little and point you in the direction of a few cool things. Have fun!

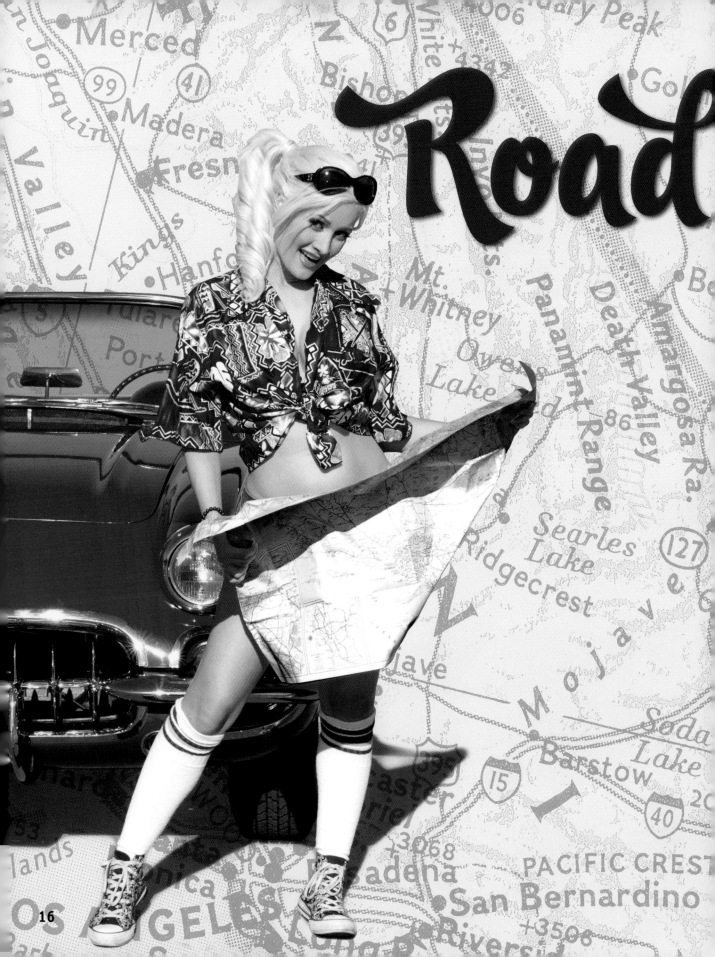

Chapter One

Trippin'

A large percentage of Las Vegas' visitors come from the Los Angeles area via automobile. In fact, if it weren't for Los Angeles patronage, Las Vegas as we know it today would probably not even exist.

Back in the 1930s, several glamorous gaming establishments dotted Los Angeles' Sunset Strip, where Hollywood stars and glitterati could drink, dance, and gamble. With the election of L.A. Mayor Fletcher Brown in 1938, everything changed. The gaming establishments on the Strip were shut down, leaving gaming operators to migrate to Las Vegas, where they could operate legally. The trend at the time was to build resorts on what then was Highway 90, the road coming into Vegas from L.A. When *Hollywood Reporter* publisher and nightclub owner Billy Wilkerson came to Las Vegas in 1945 to start building what would become the Flamingo, he nicknamed the stretch of highway "The Strip," after the L.A. landmark.

Gamblers started coming in droves from Los Angeles. Having done the drive from L.A. to Vegas many times, and knowing how hot, long and desolate it can seem now, I always think of the travelers in the 1940s and '50s and wonder how in the hell they did it. I can't imagine driving a mid-20th-century vehicle (I own a 1960 Corvette, so I know how finicky they can be — particularly that model) in the heat. Back in the days of no air conditioning and few roadside concessions, I just can't fathom how the travelers kept cool, hydrated and sane during the journey.

Today, the drive can actually be fun — and an adventure in itself — because so many quirky things have popped up along Interstate 15 over the years. I decided to investigate by doing a road trip — not to get from L.A. to Vegas or vice-versa, but for the sole purpose of investigating fun diversions along the way.

First, I would recommend driving on weekdays, if you can. A Friday afternoon drive to Las Vegas can be brutal, because that's when most Californians make the trip and traffic can get pretty rough, turning the normally four-hour drive into one as long as seven hours. The same goes for driving back on a Sunday, of course.

Several towns bleed into one another on the eastern outskirts of Los Angeles, so shopping centers, restaurants and even miniature golf can easily be found near the interstate during the first hour of the drive. The landscape really starts to get barren after that, and once past the town of Barstow, California, you are officially deep into the desert.

About halfway to Las Vegas from Los Angeles, near the town of Yermo, you may notice the word "Calico" atop a mountain in white. This moniker hovers above a re-constructed ghost town about five minutes off the interstate. It's a fun, mini-theme-park diversion in the middle of the long drive through the desert.

The charming re-creation of the mining town that stood on the spot in the 19th century was created by

Walter Knott, of Knott's Berry Farm fame, in the 1950s. The original mining town (population 3,500) was destroyed by fire in 1887, but remnants of building foundations can still be seen, such as in the Chinatown area, which originally housed forty people of Chinese origin.

A train ride runs along the ghost town, narrated by the character Hardrock John, who points out landmarks and gives passengers some Calico history. A "mystery house" offers gravity-defying illusions; gift shops offer souvenirs and photo-op cutouts line the main street. Despite obvious modern theme-park amenities, Calico remains quaint, quiet, and peaceful compared to most commercial family attractions.

Panning for gold is another fun Calico pastime. Every potential prospector is given a metal pan to dip into the cold running water and shown how to pan through the silt, looking for gold. Each person is given a little bag of fool's gold as a souvenir for his or her efforts, and the cold water is refreshing on a hot, dry desert day. If you have time, take a sepia-toned Old West photograph. Definitely don't miss the walk-through mine attraction, The Glory Tunnel, a faux mine shaft complete with a diorama depicting mining camp life in the 19th century.

Calico Ghost Town is open from 9 a.m. to 5 p.m. daily,

CALICO GHOST TOWN

1881 *Largest silver mining camp in California* 1896

with some attractions closed Mondays through Wednesdays. Admission at the time of publication was $6 for adults, $3 for children 6 through 15 and free for those 5 and younger.

You need move up only sixty years or so to dine in Yermo. Peggy Sue's '50s Diner is a large multi-room restaurant and gift shop built around the original 1954 roadside diner/truck stop. The original room has nine counter stools and three booths and usually is brimming

with regulars who come in for the fried pickles and banana-split pie, plus retro-uniformed waitresses and sometimes even the gregarious, diminutive Peggy Sue herself.

A large five-and-dime souvenir store and a pizza parlor surround the diner. Behind them is a garden with large metal dinosaur and gorilla sculptures, adding to the roadside novelty. Shade trees and water features make the "diner-saur" garden a nice place to get out and stretch after a long drive.

Since I'm a water-park enthusiast and general kid-at-heart adventurer, one of the

roadside sights that intrigued me most during my many drives between L.A. and Las Vegas was what appeared to be an abandoned water park.

Approximately 100 yards northwest of Interstate 15 in Newberry Springs, California, the haunting remains taunted my travel buddies and me every time we drove by. We would imagine stopping and exploring but never did, as we were always on too tight of a schedule.

Not surprisingly, on a drive that desolate, the boneyard-of-fun that is the abandoned water park is quite the attention-catcher. It served as a setting on *MTV's Rob and Big* show, where professional skateboarder Rob Dyrdek and friends took over the park ruins, temporarily turning them into a makeshift

The "diner-saur" garden a nice place to get out and stretch after a long drive

skate park after spotting them from the windows of a party bus on the way to Las Vegas.

Sadly, the dry waterslides so cleverly used as skate ramps are no longer, having been dismantled in 2009. Lots of the park remains still stand, however, so it makes for some interesting exploring if you are fortunate enough to gain access. The buildings have been heavily vandalized and coyotes are said to roam the property, so the place has a deliciously creepy vibe that was really fun to explore.

What remains on the grounds are some of the smaller waterslides, a dry lazy river (it was reportedly the world's longest lazy river when the park operated), some buildings painted in a '50s rock-n-roll retro style, and the concrete bases of the former large waterslides, left to stand like a baby Stonehenge.

What the cement blocks stand testament to is what was not just a water park, but quite possibly the first and most exciting water park in the world. It started as a man-made lake built by a local businessman who named it Dolores, after his wife. More and more slides were added, and the park included extraordinary attractions featuring zip-line and trapeze elements, where the riders were launched into the water. Speed slides, bumper boats and a personal-watercraft racetrack rounded out the selection of attractions at the park then named for the lake.

The park changed hands (and names) twice before closing, first becoming the '50s-themed Rock-a-Hoola water park in 1998 and then Discovery Waterpark in 2002. It closed in 2004, reportedly because of bankruptcy.

Everyone seems to notice the weird sign farther up the interstate: Zzyzx Road. The strange name came from an eccentric Los Angeles radio evangelist named Curtis "Doc" Springer. In 1944, Springer created the Zzyzx Mineral Springs and Health Spa, inventing the unusual name Zzyzx (pronounced "zeye-zicks") as "the last word in the English language." The enterprising Springer bottled the spring water from his site and sold it to parched travelers along what was then a dusty desert road.

Federal agents arrested Springer in 1974 and the government seized the property. Two years later, work began to convert it into California State University's Desert Studies Center.

At the junction of Interstate 15 and Death Valley Road is the small roadside town of Baker, California. Baker is about an hour and a half from Las Vegas and a perfect place to stop for a bite to eat. One of the most popular pit stops along the L.A.-to-Vegas drive is The Mad Greek, a kitschy little cafe surrounded by small plaster statues and offering Greek, American and Mexican fare. A particularly talked-about menu item is their excellent strawberry shake.

The most famous Baker attraction is the World's Largest Thermometer. Constructed of 33 tons of steel and filled with concrete so it won't blow over (as it did even before it was dedicated in 1991), the thermometer marks the gateway to Death Valley and is visible for miles around at a towering 134 feet, the

height symbolic of the record-setting high temperature of 134 degrees recorded in Death Valley in 1913. Constructed by the Young Electric Sign Company of Las Vegas (now known as YESCO) and using almost 5,000 bulbs to illuminate displays on all three sides of the thermometer, the landmark towers over a Bob's Big Boy Restaurant.

Nearby, just under the shadow of the largest phallic symbol in Baker, lurks the delightfully retro Bun Boy Motel sign. Ahhhh, Baker, you never fail to disappoint!

After enjoying a break in this quintessential truck stop you can hop back on Interstate 15, which will lead you straight to Las Vegas. Or, you can veer off the beaten path and take State Road 127, otherwise known as Death Valley Road. The ominously named road will extend your trip by at least two hours and lead

you to a number of colorful locations.

About an hour and a half from Baker on Death Valley Road lies the ghostly outpost of Death Valley Junction. Formerly known as Amargosa, which means "bitter waters," the junction is notable for a haunted hotel owned by an eccentric performer.

The long, single-story Spanish-style building that dominates Death Valley Junction winds along a block and surrounds a grassy courtyard. The building was constructed in 1924 to serve as a miniature city for workers of the Pacific Coast Borax Company. Inside what is now the Amargosa Hotel was a doctor's office, a hospital, boarding houses, a store, recreation hall, a dining area and, making the place even creepier, a morgue. Today the building functions as a hotel and opera house.

What the no-frills accommodations of the Amargosa may lack in amenities, they make up for in spooks. Several rooms reportedly are haunted, including Room 20, with its mysterious shaking bed, and Room 17, with the voice of a womanizing former resident. Guests in Room 15 have been said to hear a disembodied baby's voice.

An abandoned wing, now used for storage, is a creepy place I was lucky enough to be able to explore. It's a hall full of former boarding rooms, now in various states of disrepair.

At the end of the building is a small auditorium called the Amargosa Opera House, where for years proprietress Marta Becket performed, whether an audience had assembled or not.

After Ms. Becket acquired the Amargosa in 1967,

she busily devoted herself to restoring the old opera house, bringing seats in from an old Boulder City theater and spending more than four years painting an "audience" on the walls, including depictions of two of her cats, Tuxedo and Rhubarb.

In 2009, when she decided she would no longer dance en pointe at the age of 85, she launched a collaboration with friend Sandy Scheller, a mime and professional dancer. The current show includes video of Ms. Becket talking about the murals, with Scheller performing on stage.

But if you choose to bypass the ghosts and take the direct route along Interstate 15 to Las Vegas, about an hour later you will know you are approaching the border of Nevada when you reach the not-so-proper Primm, home of Buffalo Bill's and Whiskey Pete's casinos.

Formerly known as State Line, Primm straddles the border of California and Nevada, so it's the one place you can gamble in Nevada on one side of town and buy a California lottery ticket on the other. Supposedly, more California lottery tickets are sold in Primm than anywhere else in the state.

It may not sound like much when I point out the gas station in Primm — across from McDonald's — that houses a Starbucks, large public restrooms and a generously sized convenience store, but after you've been on the road for hours, trust me; you will find this place a wonderland, too! Check it out!

The most colorful property in Primm, Buffalo Bill's Resort & Casino, is a 1,200-room Wild West-themed compound complete with a buffalo-shaped pool. Winding around and through the property is the Desperado roller coaster, one of the fastest and tallest coasters in the world! The coaster only operates on weekends, though, so plan your

trip accordingly. Other attractions include an arcade, a log flume ride and more.

Whiskey Pete's Hotel & Casino is named for the most notorious character in Primm's history. In the 1920s, a gas station in Primm (the then-named State Line), was owned by one Pete McIntyre. When the gas station wasn't paying the bills, Pete resorted to bootlegging and soon earned the nickname "Whiskey Pete."

According to local lore, before Whiskey Pete passed away from miner's lung in 1933, he had requested to be buried standing up with a bottle of his signature whiskey in his hand. Years later, when a bridge connecting Whiskey Pete's Casino to Buffalo Bill's was being constructed, Whiskey Pete's body was accidentally uncovered during some digging. It has since been moved, supposedly to one of the local caves where Pete used to ply his bootlegging trade.

The last sign of civilization to be found before reaching Las Vegas is Jean, Nevada, home of the Gold Strike Casino. The "Nevada Landing" sign opposite the Gold Strike on the other side of the highway is the last standing relic of the Nevada Landing Hotel and Casino, which was shaped like a riverboat. Originally, the site was home to Jean's first casino, Pop's Oasis. When the Nevada Landing was built, chips from Pop's were dumped into the concrete foundation. After the Nevada Landing was demolished in 2008, casino chips could still be found in the foundation's concrete.

Fear and Loathing

Fear and Loathing in Las Vegas, one of the most beloved books on Las Vegas, was published in 1971 and quickly became a cult classic. Made into a just-as-beloved film starring Johnny Depp and Benicio Del Toro, author Hunter S. Thompson's drug-addled magazine-assignment-gone-awry captured the quirkiest and craziest of Las Vegas in the early '70s.

Sadly, many of the actual places visited and written about by Thompson have been imploded, demolished or redesigned, so fans can't really retrace Thompson's steps. But a few spots remain, so if you are interested in checking them out, here they are:

Bat Country: The drive to Las Vegas from Los Angeles is just as dry and hot and nearly as desolate as it was in Thompson's day. It doesn't take much imagination to think you see bats "somewhere around Barstow on the edge of the desert."

The Mint Hotel: Put up at the Mint Hotel to cover the Mint 400 dirt-bike race for **Rolling Stone** magazine, Thompson recounted his crazy adventures and exorbitant room-service bill from room 1850. The Mint no longer exists as such, but has been annexed and turned into part of Binion's on Fremont Street downtown. Perhaps, if you encounter a particularly knowledgeable staff member, he or she can show you which was room 1850 back in 1971.

The Mint Gun Club: The Mint Gun Club is no longer. It is now known as the Clark County Shooting Park, 11357 North Decatur Boulevard.

The Landmark Hotel: The Landmark Hotel is no longer. A sign from it still stands, though, behind the Riviera.

The Desert Inn: Thompson and his attorney supposedly crashed a Debbie Reynolds show at the D.I., which is no longer there, having been imploded so the Wynn Las Vegas resort could be built on the property.

Circus Circus: Circus Circus is by far the best spot for having your own Fear and Loathing experience. The casino is a bit dingy, sure, but I love that it is so similar, if not identical, to how it was in the '70s. The Carousel Bar Thompson drank at is still there, though it sells ice cream now. Wacky and surreal, with live circus performances going on above the casino floor, Circus Circus is definitely worth checking out!

Wild Bill's Cafe: I have been unable to find a Wild Bill's Cafe (alternately referred to in the book as Wild Bill's Tavern), past or present, on the outskirts of Las Vegas. If anyone out there tracks it down, please let me know! The same goes for The Big Flip Diner.

Majestic Diner: There is no Majestic Diner, renowned for its seafood or otherwise, in Baker, California. You are better off looking for The Mad Greek.

Flamingo Hotel: Thompson's second writing assignment was to cover the district attorney's convention. For this assignment he was put up at the Flamingo, which still stands on the corner of Las Vegas Boulevard South and Flamingo Road although, due to remodeling projects, I doubt mini-suite 1150 is still there.

The Dunes: Thompson's fictionalized alter ego, Raoul Duke, attended the "Third National Institute on Narcotics and Dangerous Drugs" at the Dunes, which was imploded and replaced by the Bellagio on the Strip.

The North Star Coffee Lounge: According to local lore, The North Star Coffee Lounge actually is the North Vegas Diner, 5150 North Camino Al Norte in North Las Vegas.

Las Vegas Hi

Watch any of the major documentaries made on Las Vegas in the '90s and one of the first things brought up is the oddity of such a major city out in the middle of the desert. The talking heads wonder: "Why would anyone come here? Why does this city exist?"

True, from today's vantage point, a city like Las Vegas (large, over-the-top, luxurious, and excessively consumerist), standing lonely in the middle of what seems like a barren desert — and with growth patterns that have threatened to exceed available resources — seems to make no sense.

In reality, it was Vegas' water supply, namely its two springs, which attracted settlers in the first place. From the Paiute tribes to Spanish traders, mapmakers, Mormon missionaries, and railroad magnates, many people saw the Vegas valley as an ideal stop on the way from Salt Lake City to Los Angeles. The aquifer in the middle of the desert not only attracted settlers but also gave Las Vegas its name, which is Spanish for "the Meadows."

Bridging the gap between those who passed through on the emigrant trail and those who settled here after the 1905 land auction that would establish Las Vegas as the city it is today was the soap opera that was the life of Helen Stewart.

story

My favorite first lady of Las Vegas, massive overachiever and drama magnet Helen Stewart arrived in the valley from Pioche, Nevada, in 1882. Her husband, Archibald, held the mortgage on a ranch owned by settler Octavius Decatur Gass, and Gass had defaulted.

Two years later, on a day when Archibald Stewart was away on business, ranch hand Schuyler Henry told Helen he was quitting and demanded his pay. After she told him he'd have to the await the return of her husband, he verbally abused her and defected to the Kiel Ranch in what is now North Las Vegas.

Shortly after his return, Archibald Stewart set out to confront Henry. Back in the days of the Old West, a situation like this often involved firearms and, hours later, Mrs. Stewart learned her husband was dead. Pregnant with her fifth child, she was stuck retrieving her husband's body herself and burying him in a coffin made out of two of her ranch's wooden doors.

As if that weren't dramatic enough, the law found no proof to convict whomever killed Mr. Stewart. He died without a will,

Helen Stewart, first lady of Las Vegas. (Right) Senator William Clark, who bought Stewart's ranch, waves from his train.

so Helen faced a legal battle to get ownership of the ranch.

And Helen's troubles wouldn't end anytime soon. Archie — the child with whom she had been pregnant when her husband was killed — died before his fifteenth birthday after falling from a horse. And later the Kiel sons, Ed and William, were found dead on their ranch by Helen's fiancé and his son. Though the cause of death was ruled a murder-suicide at the time, a later examination of the bodies deemed it a double murder. Possible vengeance, putting any Hatfield-McCoy drama

to shame? The world may never know.

Perhaps the only things more astounding than the drama in Helen's life are her accomplishments. Left to run a 1,000-acre ranch on her own in the middle of a desert in the early 1900s, she also became a postmistress, ran a rest stop for weary travelers, became a public speaker, was the first woman elected to the Clark County school board, and raised five children.

After selling a portion of her land in 1902, she built new homes in Las Vegas and Los Angeles and gave ten acres of

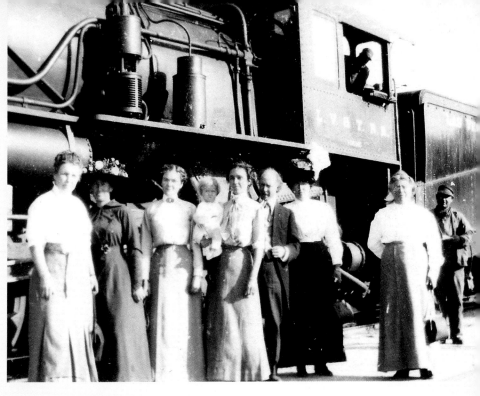

(Above) Properly dressed Las Vegas ladies wait for a train about 1906. (Below) Tents were the first buildings in Las Vegas, accommodations have improved somewhat since then.

her land to the Paiute Indians (who still have it today). She also founded the Mesquite Club, the first women's organization in Las Vegas.

Railroads and Red Lights

When Helen Stewart finally sold most of her land, it was for $55,000 to a senator from Montana, a whiskered, corrupt copper-baron-turned-politician named William Clark. Clark was then building a railroad line from Salt Lake City to Los Angeles and, like explorers and traders before him, saw Las Vegas as the perfect pit stop between the two cities. Since steam engines need water to operate, the Vegas Valley (then with a population of around thirty) and its two aquifers seemed the ideal place to put the railroad stop and the repair shops needed for operation.

Clark heavily advertised an auction of the parcels of his newly purchased land that he wished to sell, and people looking to relocate and bring business to Las Vegas flocked to the area. They pitched tents and

(Left) The Arizona Club, Las Vegas' first luxury (and all male) social. (Right) "Working girls" relax in front of the Arizona Club in block 16 the "red light" district. (Below) "Chop Houses" supplied boxed, chopped dinners to train travelers—the first fast food to-go.

awaited the land auction, which turned out to be a huge success for Clark, who made five times what he had paid Helen Stewart for the land.

The first major "buildings" in Las Vegas, including the first hotel and hospital, were simply large tents. As actual buildings were erected along the then-unpaved Fremont Street and in the surrounding area that now makes up downtown Las Vegas, the block surrounded by Ogden, Stewart, First and Second streets became the red-light district, full of saloons and houses of ill repute — the notorious

Block 16, named for the number assigned to it during the land auction. Las Vegas' first "luxury" establishment, the Arizona Club, was in Block 16. With a mahogany bar and electricity for special occasions, the Arizona Club earned a reputation as the fanciest bar in town.

The railroad era definitely gave Las Vegas its start as a 24-hour town, with businesses striving to cater

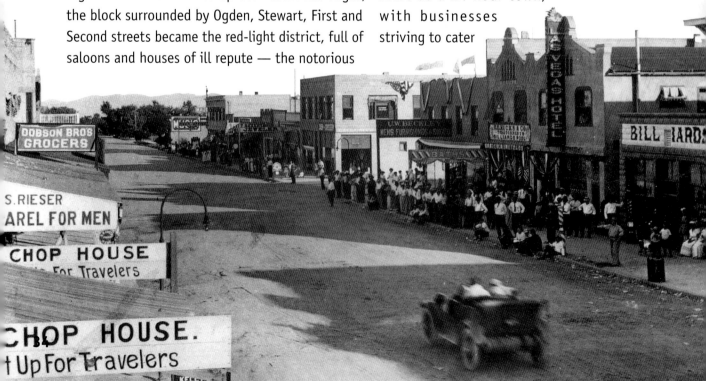

to the round-the-clock railroad schedule, as the passengers on layover were Vegas' main source of tourist income.

I can't imagine living in the Las Vegas heat back then. People didn't exactly wear skimpy outfits at the turn of the 20th century, and the "air conditioning" of the time generally consisted of pinning up a wet sheet next to you and hoping a breeze would blow through it. Despite the sometimes miserable conditions, somehow the early Las Vegans pulled through, working hard to establish what they could never have had any idea it would become: the most visited city in the world.

The Best Dam Thing to Happen to Vegas Since the Railroad

Vegas hit one of its first major stumbling blocks after World War I ended in 1917 and demand for Nevada's metal resources sharply decreased. Heavy layoffs, a nationwide railroad strike and Union Pacific's decision to move its maintenance shop from Las Vegas to Caliente, Nevada, nearly ruined the less-than-fifteen-year-old town.

What gave the city hope were the unique advantages it could offer. Lenient marriage and divorce laws, the city's gambling past, and very warm

A shortage of worker housing led to Hoover Dam workers' familes to live in tents by the river.

weather inspired some to think of Las Vegas as having potential as a tourist city.

Fortune smiled on Las Vegas in 1928, when the Boulder Canyon Project Act was signed. It was aimed at harnessing the power of the Colorado River by building a dam that would be dubbed the "eighth wonder of the world" in Black Canyon, about thirty miles from Las Vegas. Not only did tourists rush to see this wonder while it was being built, but people desperate to find jobs during the Great Depression streamed to Las Vegas. The workers who did get hired (up to 5,000 worked on the dam at a time) were housed in the newly formed Boulder City, where bans on alcohol and gambling were enforced. And so, after a hot, dangerous workday at the dam, many workers drove thirty miles north to Las Vegas to spend their hard-earned money on liquor, women, gambling and a good time.

Las Vegas's dreams of becoming a major tourist draw started to come true.

This welcome economic boom helped Las Vegas grow to a city of some 8,000 people, and dreams of it becoming a major tourist draw were starting to come true. Entrepreneurs came to Las Vegas, planting the seeds of what would eventually become an empire of mega-resort hotel/casinos. Bootlegger and "connected" guy Tony Cornero came to town to open The Meadows Club right outside the city limits — now the intersection of Fremont Street and Charleston Boulevard — in 1931, just as gambling was legalized in Nevada (after being banned twenty-one years before). Not only did The Meadows Club offer gaming, entertainment (the Meadows Revue, produced by Broadway's Jack Laughlin), dining and drinking; it also had a hotel and even its own landing strip! Despite all of the bells and whistles, The Meadows Club was not a financial success. Two months after the opening, Cornero sold the hotel, which burned down just months later.

The business model for the Vegas resort didn't die with The Meadows Club, however, as more enterprising individuals would come to town to open their own one-stop entertainment destinations.

The Birth of the Strip

After Hoover Dam was completed, Las Vegas continued to prosper. Although many of the workers left, the dam continued to attract tourists. Las Vegas reinvented itself as a Western-themed tourist destination, establishing Helldorado Days, an annual rodeo festival. Helldorado Village, a reproduction of an old Western town, was built downtown as a tourist attraction. In the early '40s, with World War II on the horizon, a gunnery school and a magnesium plant were opened in the area. By 1945, the population would be double what it had been just five years earlier.

At about this time the Las Vegas Chamber of Commerce thought it would be a good idea to bring a hotel chain to town to add to the city's tourist appeal. While the El Rancho Hotel chain's Thomas Hull was brought to Vegas and invited to build one of his hotels downtown, the enterprising Hull went elsewhere and built south of the city, along Highway 91, the road that led to Los Angeles. Hull saw more potential along the highway, where he could buy land cheaper, have more space to build and — because it was outside the city limits — avoid some taxes and building codes. Many tourists who visit Las Vegas even today are unaware that the bustling Strip hotel they are staying in is not technically in

Las Vegas, but in unincorporated Clark County.

Hull's El Rancho Vegas, which opened in 1941, was a sprawling, ranch-style building with plenty of parking, space for horseback riding, an "opera house" for entertainment, a large swimming pool, health club, shops and various dining establishments, including Las Vegas' first all-you-can-eat buffet, the Chuck Wagon. The El Rancho Vegas set the stage for the Las Vegas resort we know and love today.

Soon after the El Rancho Vegas opened, The Last Frontier, another Western-themed resort, opened on Highway 91. The owners of The Last Frontier bought the famous mahogany bar from The Arizona Club and added a miniature Western village complete with wedding chapel — The Little Church of the West, which has been moved and can still be found on the south end of the Strip, across from Mandalay Bay.

By about the mid-1940s, Billy Wilkerson — Los Angeles club owner, publisher of *The Hollywood Reporter* and inveterate gambler — came to Las Vegas with a vision for the "American Monte Carlo." He wanted to open a posh, sophisticated

HAVE FUN IN THE SUN

LAS VEGAS NEVADA

Nevada

SAN FRANCISCO

LAS VEGAS

California

LOS ANGELES

El Mirador 2200 So. Fifth
Phone-4800 Las Vegas, Nv.

gaming establishment unlike the Western-themed hotels. About that time Guy McAfee re-named Highway 91 south of Las Vegas "The Strip," after L.A.'s Sunset Strip, which was dotted by many famous clubs.

Wilkerson, with notorious gangster Benjamin "Bugsy" Siegel as a business partner (and other mobsters in the shadows), began construction on the Flamingo Hotel, named for Wilkerson's favorite bird. It was to be more luxurious than anything Las Vegas had ever seen, as well as one of the first air-conditioned hotels in town. But because of the expense of post-war materials, overbuilding because of Siegel's personal paranoia, and a huge proportion of theft, it ran way over budget. In 1947 Siegel was shot dead in his girlfriend's Beverly Hills home — a killing

Further setting the stage for Las Vegas to become a premier tourist destination was the opening of an airport named for Nevada Senator Pat McCarran, who was influential in its establishment.

that officially was never solved but generally accepted to be ordered by organized-crime figures miffed by the cost overruns. The Fabulous Flamingo was taken over by Siegel's associates and has changed hands many times over the years. It is now owned by Caesars Entertainment, Inc. and is the oldest existing resort on the Strip.

Bugsy Siegel

The Fabulous Fifties

The Flamingo was followed by the Thunderbird in 1948, and new hotels started popping up along the Strip as Las Vegas became known as a glamorous gaming getaway. The population tripled during the '50s as the industry kept creating jobs that lured new residents.

Plush desert-themed hotels like the Desert Inn, the Sahara, the Sands and the Dunes were

built along the Strip in the 1950s. The tremendous growth of Las Vegas also drew such resorts as the Riviera, the Royal Nevada, the Tropicana and the Stardust, which would set a record with its enormous sign that launched a trend of neon on the Strip. Foreshadowing the constant renovations that would go on in Strip hotels over the years was The Last Frontier, which was remodeled and reopened in 1955 as The New Frontier, trading in its cowboy theme for a Buzz Lightyear-worthy space-age motif.

Further growth ushered in the Showboat, a fancy ship-shaped hotel not downtown or on the Strip but on Boulder Highway, and the Moulin Rouge, on Bonanza Road in west Las Vegas.

The Moulin Rouge is of particular interest because it symbolizes the era of racial segregation and the subsequent integration that seemed late in coming for a city as otherwise liberal as Las Vegas.

The schizophrenic nature in which people of color were treated in Las Vegas is perhaps best symbolized by a black entertainer's typical stay in the city during this era. The biggest entertainers of the day were offered top dollar to perform in Las Vegas hotels, luring in patrons who would no doubt drop some money on the gaming tables. These

entertainers included Sammy Davis Jr., Nat King Cole, Lena Horne, and Dorothy Dandridge.

Typically, an entertainer headlining at a Vegas hotel — then as now — would be put up in one of the most posh suites the establishment had to offer. In the '50s, though, black entertainers were for the most part not welcomed in the hotels and had to seek lodging in boarding houses in west Las Vegas, where most of the city's black residents lived.

When the first integrated hotel and casino was opened on the west side, it was a runaway hit. The Moulin Rouge offered drinks, lodging, gambling and entertainment to people of every color. The luxury establishment added a third late show to its entertainment roster, and it wasn't long before all Strip entertainers, black and white, were flocking to the Moulin Rouge after hours.

Unfortunately, the new hottest spot in Las Vegas closed less than a year after it opened, under mysterious circumstances. The Moulin Rouge's last and most significant hurrah took place on March 25, 1960, when city leaders met there to create an agreement to desegregate hotels and casinos in Las Vegas.

An offbeat testament to Las Vegas' unique and enduring ingenuity was the use of nearby atomic testing as a tourist attraction during the '50s. When the federal government set up a testing site just sixty-five miles from Las Vegas, it could have been seen as a true disaster for tourism. Instead, it became an attraction as bars promoted "atomic cocktails," hotels hosted mushroom-cloud-viewing parties, and postcards, like one from Binion's Horseshoe Club, carried photos of atomic blasts. Perhaps the campiest embrace of the atomic test site was "Miss Atomic Bomb" a beauty photographed in a mushroom-cloud-bedecked bathing suit.

The Swinging Sixties

The '60s in Las Vegas were virtually defined by Frank Sinatra and the Rat Pack. When Sinatra, Sammy Davis Jr., Dean Martin, and Joey Bishop were brought to Las Vegas to film the movie *Ocean's Eleven* in 1960, a new identity for the city was born. After filming the movie during the day, the boys would head over to the Sands and put on a show in the Copa Room, becoming the hottest act in town overnight. The group performance was initially dubbed "The Summit," but the guys together would come to be known as the "Rat Pack", a group nickname bestowed on them by Humphrey Bogart's wife, Lauren Bacall, when they hung out at her place in Los Angeles.

The star-studded show at the Sands became legendary not only for packing the house every night but also for drawing a star-studded audience. If you were lucky enough to see the Rat Pack at The Sands, you just may have been sitting next to Marilyn Monroe, a Kennedy or Elizabeth Taylor.

The sophisticated, "ring-a-ding-ding" cool of the Rat Pack became synonymous with Vegas

The '60s in Las Vegas were virtually defined by the 'Rat Pack.'

style, as did the style of Elvis Presley when *Viva Las Vegas* was released in 1964, starring Elvis and Ann-Margret. Elvis would marry his sweetheart, Priscilla Beaulieu, at the Aladdin in 1967.

Another shift in Las Vegas' image came after the arrival of the world's first billionaire, Howard Hughes, in 1966. Hughes was so wealthy that he had to make some investments so he could avoid the huge taxes that came with large amounts of dormant money. Vegas soon became his personal game of Monopoly as

(Above) Viva Las Vegas! Ann Margaret and Elvis. (Below) Howard Hughes dabbled in film before coming to Las Vegas.

(Clockwise from top left) There's craps floating in the Sands pool! Ike and Tina Turner. The Stardust and its Lido de Paris, Hughes's Landmark tower of failure.

he bought loads of real estate, starting with the Desert Inn. After being threatened with eviction after a long stay in a high-roller suite at the D.I., Hughes simply offered to buy the joint.

After the Desert Inn, Hughes purchased the Frontier, the Sands, the Silver Slipper, the Landmark, and the Castaways, along with massive amounts of undeveloped land in the area.

Hughes was well into his eccentric phase in the mid-1960s and, despite never leaving his room and refusing to allow a background check or to be photographed or fingerprinted, was granted a difficult-to-get Nevada gaming license, allowing him to own casinos. Why was the Gaming Control Board so lax with Hughes? Because he was a well known, non-mob-associated, respected billionaire. Up to this point, most major building projects in Las Vegas were funded by mob money or Teamster pension funds, also wrangled by the mob. The arrival of Hughes marked a change in Las Vegas' reputation and started a movement that would lead to most of the major casinos in town being owned by publicly held corporations.

The Corporate Era

Everything seemed to get bigger and better in Las Vegas in the '60s and '70s. Jay Sarno opened two themed resorts, Caesars Palace and Circus Circus, both of which became classics and are still thriving on the Strip today. Multi-millionaire Kirk Kerkorian opened the largest hotels in the world — the International Hotel (now the Las Vegas Hilton), on

Paradise Road just east of the Strip and the MGM Grand, on the corner of Flamingo Road and Las Vegas Boulevard South (now Bally's). The International would become renowned for its entertainment, at one time offering Ike and Tina Turner, the Broadway musical *Hair* and Elvis Presley all performing in the hotel's showrooms. At the International from 1969 to 1977, Elvis performed a total of 837 sold-out

shows, becoming one of the most classic and popular symbols of Las Vegas.

On television, Aaron Spelling's *Vega$*, a detective drama starring Robert Urich, brought the campy glamour of Las Vegas into the homes of millions of Americans every week. Urich's character drove a cool vintage Thunderbird, lived in a fantasy drive-in bachelor pad, and was constantly surrounded by beautiful women. The show was a success, lasting three seasons, and was the first major television show produced entirely in Las Vegas.

The Birth of the Mega-Resort

Las Vegas went through a slump in the '80s. First, two tragic hotel fires earned it the nickname "Singed City." The first, at the MGM Grand on November 21, 1980, killed eighty-five people and injured hundreds more. It was followed three months later by a fire at the International in which eight people died. Meanwhile, the 1977 legalization of gambling in Atlantic City, New Jersey, was stealing countless potential Las Vegas visitors.

While Vegas in the '80s may have appeared at first glance to be an aging, tacky image of its former cool, a brighter future was brewing at the Golden Nugget. After making some shrewd real-estate investments, Steve Wynn bought a controlling interest in the Nugget, located downtown, which for many years had been overshadowed by the Strip. The Nugget was in need of a massive

(Left) Kirk Kerkorian, (below left) the original MGM Grand burns, (right) The Mirage drew a crowd on opening day in 1989, and (far right) Steve Wynn.

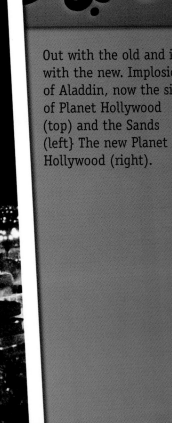

Out with the old and in with the new. Implosions of Aladdin, now the site of Planet Hollywood (top) and the Sands (left} The new Planet Hollywood (right).

48

makeover, which it got. Wynn also added a four-star hotel tower and hired Frank Sinatra to perform in the showroom. Television commercials from the 1980s starred Wynn himself and showed off the luxurious rooms, restaurants and lobby — and in some, even Sinatra made a cameo. At the end of one of the Nugget commercials, Wynn's face popped up on the Nugget's marquee as he said, "We're going to make Las Vegas famous!" This may have seemed like a goofy, bombastic line at the time, but making Las Vegas even more famous than it already was exactly what Wynn did when he opened the Mirage in 1989.

After the success of the revamped Golden Nugget and the opening of a Golden Nugget in Atlantic City, Wynn secured financing for his new vision for Las Vegas. What he envisioned was a destination in itself, more than just a typical hotel/casino. The Mirage, still one of the star resorts on the Strip, opened as the largest hotel in the world with a gorgeous nine-story atrium housing a tropical rainforest in the center of the entryway. The tropical-themed resort has a beautiful 20,000-gallon saltwater aquarium behind the check-in counter, the Secret Garden filled with exotic animals, and a dolphin training program. In front of the hotel, right on the Strip, a man-made volcano erupts every half-hour, not only drawing crowds but also making the typical wait for a valeted car an experience. Wynn's gamble paid off as The Mirage surpassed Hoover Dam as the state's most-visited tourist attraction only a year after it opened.

The Theme Era

The Mirage led to an explosion of new, hyper-themed, family-friendly, Disneyland-for-adults megaresorts up and down the Strip. The next was the Excalibur, a massive, King-Arthur-themed resort with a castle-like building surrounded by a moat complete with an animatronics dragon.

Next came the Egyptian-themed Luxor pyramid hotel, with Nile River-style boat rides (which no longer exist) running through it, and Wynn's pirate-themed Treasure Island, where resident pirate ships engage in mock battles every night. The new MGM Grand opened in 1993 as an Emerald City with Wizard of Oz figures inside and a theme park on the back lot. Bob Stupak's Stratosphere, the largest freestanding tower west of the Mississippi, opened in 1996. It looks a lot like Seattle's Space Needle, but with a hotel and casino at its base and a restaurant, lounge and thrill rides on its top. The New York, New York resort brought a miniature version of the Big Apple to Las Vegas' Strip and has a Coney-Island-style roller coaster wrapping around the property. Theming resorts was so popular in the '90s and defined Las Vegas so much that a Sands Hotel PR spokeswoman, addressing a planned renovation, told *Time* magazine, "We are going to theme, definitely, but we don't know what the themes are yet."

The family-friendly trend in Las Vegas eventually fell out of favor. All of the properties mentioned in the past two paragraphs still exist, but many of them have been restyled in more sophisticated

Family-friendly Las Vegas eventually fell out of favor.

ways. The MGM Grand shows no trace of its Wizard of Oz past except for the emerald color of the building itself. Instead, it is known for Las Vegas' largest nightclub, Studio 54, top-notch gourmet restaurants and a variety of shows. Wet Republic, a party pool, now stands where the amusement park used to be. If you peer over the concrete wall separating the ultra-pool from the limo parking lot, you can still see some fairy-tale-style buildings left over from the park.

Luxury Las Vegas

As a lure to high rollers and the bourgeoisie alike, luxury became a new focus of the Las Vegas innovator of the late '90s. To make way for the luxury establishments to come, old ones had to be razed, and in true Las Vegas fashion they went out with a showy bang. The engineered implosions of old hotels became bittersweet events in Las Vegas, saying goodbye to the old and making way for the new. Old standards like the Sands, the Desert Inn, and the Dunes were done away with. The destruction of the Dunes was even orchestrated to appear to be triggered by a blast from one of Treasure Island's pirate ships, adding to the spectacle of the moment.

In place of these desert-themed oldies rose some of the most luxurious resorts ever seen in Las Vegas.

Perhaps best symbolizing Las Vegas' embrace of new luxury is the Bellagio. When it opened in 1998, the Bellagio was the most expensive hotel ever built. The region surrounding Italy's Lake Como inspired its elegant look. The lobby ceiling is covered in a rainbow of Dale Chihuly's blown-glass flowers, and the amazing Conservatory and Botanical Gardens must be seen to be believed. Cirque du Soleil's stunning *O* is the resident show. The refined elegance the Bellagio brought to Las Vegas also is reflected in its art gallery and the collection of works by Picasso in the restaurant of the same name.

And the man-made lake in front of the resort, with the Fountains of Bellagio, has become a new Las Vegas icon, as frequently photographed as the "Welcome to Las Vegas" sign.

In place of the Sands came The Venetian, the gilded replica of Venice, Italy, with gondola rides, luxury shopping and breathtaking decor. In place of the Desert Inn rose Wynn's eponymous resort, Wynn Las Vegas, and its sister property, Encore, two of the most luxurious resorts on the Strip today.

Luxury shopping centers such as The Forum Shops at Caesars, super-sized entertainment venues like the Coliseum at Caesars Palace, rooms run by celebrity chefs and upscale dining and residential areas such as Lake Las Vegas changed the image of Las

Vegas once again as a world-class destination, a place to spend as much as you wished in the midst of the thriving economy of the 1990s.

Everybody Loves Las Vegas

Vegas grew to even greater popularity with the appeal it gained with a younger demographic, starting when the Hard Rock Hotel opened in 1995. A rock-themed casino with the risqué Sunday pool party Rehab, fun restaurants like the Pink Taco and displays of rock memorabilia, it became the go-to hangout for the young.

The city's appeal grew even

more with the opening of the Palms in 2001. Clean, modern design, a location close to but off the Strip and constant celebrity sightings and TV exposure made the Palms an instant hit. Owner George Maloof's unique approach to attract the younger crowd worked. MTV's *The Real World* filmed there in 2002 and the modern luxury suite designed for the reality show became available for guests after filming wrapped. Though celebrities frequent most major resorts in Vegas, celebrity moments had a way of becoming synonymous with the Palms. Britney Spears was staying at the Palms when she infamously got married for fifty-five hours in 2004, even taking a green Palms limo to the wedding chapel. Jessica Simpson reportedly owns a condo in Palms Place. Hugh Hefner has a suite and a Playboy Club in the Palms' Fantasy Tower. Most of Katy Perry's "Waking Up in Vegas" music video takes place at the Palms.

In lieu of typical Vegas shows, the Hard Rock and the Palms both have concert venues where the hottest acts in music play, as well as multiple nightclubs.

Nightclub culture really took off in Vegas in the early 2000s. Today it's hard to imagine Vegas without nightclubs, but the boom didn't really start until a

(Clockwise from left) Cirque du Soleil's *Mysteré*; the Bellagio fountains; the Encore marquee; the Beach Club at Encore; (background) Chihuly art glass ceiling at Bellagio.

little less than ten years ago. Now almost every resort has a club and an ultra-lounge. Celebrity hosts and DJs are paid big money to host evenings at nightclubs, a practice that peaked on New Year's Eve 2008, when Pamela Anderson was allegedly paid $1 million to host at Pure at Caesars Palace.

To resort owners, revenues from hotel rooms, entertainment, and drinks became as important as the profits made on the casino floor. People were coming to Vegas more than ever for the total experience, not just to gamble. Shows on the Strip were becoming bigger and more elaborate, expected to be profit centers in themselves and not just loss leaders, as they had been in the past. By 2009 there were seven big-budget Cirque du Soleil spectaculars on the Strip. Vegas was more popular than ever, surpassing Mecca as the world's most-visited city in 1999.

(Clockwise from upper left) Palms Hotel Casino; George Maloof and Lady Gaga, The Kardashians host a party at Tao; Rehab pool party at Hard Rock hotel.

Great Recession and Recovery

When the housing market plummeted in September 2008, the country was plunged into the worst economic crisis since the Great Depression. Due to Las Vegas' dependence on disposable income and tourist dollars, the city tends to be hit harder than anywhere else during an economic downturn, seeing the effects of the slump sooner and taking longer than many places to recover. While months earlier the city was so brimming with construction projects that locals joked that the state bird should be the crane — as in construction crane — it ground to a virtual halt. Numerous large-scale projects on the Strip were left standing in various states of completion.

Many thought Vegas had seen its best days. Foreclosure rates were abominably high, as so many had thought of Vegas as the perfect place to buy a new home, investment property or vacation condo in the early part of the decade.

But Las Vegans can always be counted on for their ingenuity and ability to reinvent their city during tough times. CityCenter opened in late 2009, adding to the Strip a gorgeous complex filled with multi-million dollars worth of art and some of the highest-end lodgings and shopping in the city. The Encore resort in 2010 added the Strip's most plush pool yet, which was an instant hit. Visitation is back up again after the slump of the past few years, proving, yet again, that Las Vegas is here to stay.

(Clockwise from above) Aria hotel and casino in City Center; Las Vegas' newest hotel and casino, The Cosmopolitan, City Center; in front of the Frank Gehry-designed Cleveland Clinic Lou Ruvo Center for Brain Health.

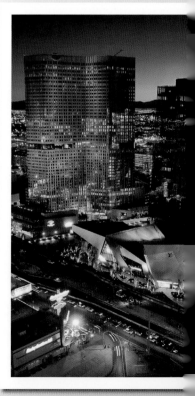

THE COSMOPOLITAN

Chapter Three

Suite Dreams

Las Vegas is home to some of the most luxurious hotels in the world. Even bargain-rate rooms are available inside multi-billion-dollar resorts, but few people get to see the hotels' high-roller suites — spots so exclusive that they often don't have price tags but are bestowed on high rollers, VIPs and celebrities during their stays, at management's discretion. For example, at The Mirage, higher-roller villas are located past a security gate at the end of a secret driveway tucked deep within the resort. Each villa is a lavishly decorated apartment with private butler service, mirrors over the beds, and a private backyard with pool and putting green. Unless you plan on buddying up with a celebrity or dropping copious amounts of cash on the casino floor, you will probably never stay in any of these secret suites. This chapter provides a peek inside for the curious.

(Left) Laura Croft and me on the putting green at a Mirage villa, (right) and me in front of Planet Hollywood on the day I moved in, when the sign was changed to Planet Holly for one night.

I was lucky enough to stay in the Hugh Hefner Sky Villa at the Palms several times. It's not only the ideal party suite in Vegas, but also one of the most expensive hotel rooms in the world.

Most casinos don't put a price on their high-roller suites, simply because they don't rent them by the night but only give them to high rollers who dump a ton of cash in the casino. The Hugh Hefner suite certainly is used in the same fashion, but also is available for $40,000 a night. The two-story mega-suite includes an eight-foot rotating round bed in the master bedroom, a gym, sauna, massage room, glass elevator and a patio with an infinity-edge hot tub with a fabulous view of the Strip. The two upstairs bedrooms overlook the floor below and have sliding glass doors so one has the option of privacy or to be part of the party downstairs. On the lower floor are a media room, dining room, kitchen, and living area that open onto the patio. Additional bedrooms connect to the suite, as anyone willing to shell out $40,000 for the night is probably rolling with a colossal crew.

Believe it or not, I have probably only stayed the night in the suite once or twice, because when I was traveling with Hef and the girls, our busy schedules usually prevented sleeping over. If you ask me, though, the suite is the

perfect place to have an after-party late into the morning.

One of the most gigantic suites I have seen in Las Vegas is the Hardwood Suite in the Palms Fantasy Tower. The Maloof family, owners of the Palms, also own the Sacramento Kings basketball team, so their team color purple adorns the half basketball court (yes, basketball court) in the suite. The 10,000-square-foot, two-story party palace also includes a scoreboard, pool table, bar, dining area and living room. The beds are Murphy beds that pull out from the walls onto the basketball court and yes, they are extra-long — the perfect size for pro basketball players (or those who would like to pretend for a night). It's a great place to throw a party, as there's nothing more fun than trying to make a free throw while intoxicated.

Formerly the Hot Pink Suite, where my buddy

Stacey had her bachelorette party on *The Girls Next Door*, the premier bachelorette pad in Las Vegas is now the Palms' Barbie Suite, with decor by Jonathan Adler. Built to celebrate the 50th anniversary of the Barbie doll in 2009, the suite was designed with Barbie's image everywhere in the pink, black and lime-green playroom. With its own bar, extra-large living/dining area and bedroom with Jacuzzi tub and fireplace, it's the perfect spot for a girl to relax, party — or a little bit of both.

If the Barbie suite is perfect for a bachelorette party, its bachelor counterpart would have to be the Erotic Suite, also in

the Palms Fantasy Tower. Decorated like a sexy devil's den in red and black, vinyl and stripper poles, it's the perfect place for a bachelor party or a sexy weekend away with a special someone.

One of the most fun suites at the Palms — and in all of Las Vegas — is the Kingpin Suite, which has multiple bedrooms, plus its own bowling alley in the living room. You may have seen the suite on *The Girls Next Door*, when Kendra celebrated her twenty-first birthday there. Frustrated that I couldn't bowl a strike, I bowled myself down the alley, knocking the pins down with my body and almost getting

My favorite suite at Rumor Boutique Hotel is not only decorated in my favorite color — pink — it has a balcony overlooking the hotel's pool and courtyard.

crushed by the pin grabber. Don't try that yourselves, kids!

The Absolut Suite, my favorite at Caesars Palace, has the fun, vibrant look of a reality-show house, with rooms themed around different flavors of Absolut Vodka. The immense two-story party area/living room is decorated in black and raspberry, for Absolut Raspberri. Absolut Citron inspired the yellow beach-cabana-style bedroom on the second floor, and Absolut

Peach was the inspiration for the other second-floor bedroom, which employs clever optical illusions with carpeting printed to look like a swimming pool and a bed comforter made to look like a pool float. This may be confusing if you're drunk, but I have yet to test it. The two bedrooms on the first floor are my favorite. One has bedding in a cute retro tangerine print. The Absolut Vanilla room is super-cute as well, made to look like a snowy lodge with trompe l'oeil wallpaper that gives the bathroom the appearance of a Swedish sauna, plus curtains covered in snowflakes and wooden Scandinavian furniture.

The most beautiful suite on the Strip, in my opinion, is the Napoleon Suite at Paris Las Vegas. On the thirty-first floor of the hotel, the sweeping 4,300-square-foot luxury suite feels like a Parisian apartment or top French hotel. The sumptuous nineteenth-century-style decor, grand piano, gold-plated fixtures, hardwood floors and black marble bathtubs set it apart from any in Las Vegas. There's plenty of space for travel companions in this five-bedroom, six-bath mega-suite, which not only has a living room, bar, media room and dining room, but also a private butler and massage service. The

69

Napoleon Suite is never available to the public, but exclusively reserved for high rollers.

Although most of the suites I'm profiling are wish-book-status super-expensive or impossible-to-get-your-hands-on dream suites, this chapter wouldn't be complete without a look at some of the kitschiest spots in town. The definite frontrunner in this category has to be the Elvis and Priscilla Suite at the Viva Las Vegas Wedding Chapel. North of the Strip, across from the Stratosphere on Las Vegas Boulevard South, Viva Las Vegas is chock-full of themed rooms (Gangster, Egyptian, Gothic, anyone?). But the crown jewel is the campy homage to the King, the Elvis and Priscilla Suite, featuring a bed shaped like a Pink Cadillac, Graceland painted on the walls and a bathroom with a mirror-sur-rounded hot tub. For the quirky Vegas adventurer and Elvis-phile, this suite won't disappoint.

With the best views of the Strip and a relaxing,

Zen-like atmosphere, the Mandarin Oriental is one of my favorite hotels in Las Vegas. The beautifully modern decor with Art Deco and Asian touches brings visitors into an oasis right in the middle

Fabulous Private Pool Suites

(Left), the Mandarin Suite at the Mandarin Oriental, (top) a luxury Las Vegas hotel suite, circa 1964, (above) the Tuscan villas of the secret MGM Mansions.

Also in the top-floor suite is a private pool, garden and koi pond.

The first place I ever stayed in Las Vegas is one of the city's best-kept secrets. Nestled deep in the middle of the MGM Grand complex is the MGM Mansion, an eleven-year-old structure modeled after an eighteenth-century Tuscan villa. I would never be able to get into this place on my own, as it is for "invited guests only." I was tagging along with Hef and company for a Playmate's birthday, but what a way to tag along! Entering the Mansion property feels like pulling up to a different world, far away from the typical Vegas hustle and bustle. Beautiful gardens surround the building and a glass dome covers the area, making it impervious to weather. Besides the Mansion's twenty-nine villas, each with its own indoor swimming pool, there is a private spa, casino and billiard room inside the Mansion, which is adjacent to the rest of the MGM property, should you feel the need to venture back into the real world.

The craziest suite in Vegas has to be the Provocateur Suite at the Hard Rock — a fetish-themed suite at the most risqué hotel in

of all of the action. If you want to come to Las Vegas to relax — or just momentarily escape the party — the Mandarin Suite is perfect. Its 3,100 square feet include two bedrooms, a fitness area, living room, dining room, bar, and study.

Easily snagging one of the superlative titles in Las Vegas is the Verona Suite at the Las Vegas Hilton, where Elvis stayed during his run at the hotel in the '70s. It's known as the largest in Las Vegas, at a whopping 15,000 square feet! As the name suggests, Italian-style decor is used throughout the three-bedroom suite, with intricately hand-painted ceilings and walls.

town. The must-be-seen-to-be-believed super-suite in the resort's new HRH tower boasts a bed the size of three queen-sized mattresses, with images of dancing almost-naked girls projected onto the bed. A human-sized birdcage, dungeon, whips, handcuffs, and paddles set the scene for this one-of-a-kind experience.

If you are looking for a party spot right on the Strip, one of the Planet Hollywood Apex Suites would be the best place to have a large bash, or just a small slumber party of your own. With fantastic views of the Strip and the Bellagio Fountains, the 1,900-square-foot, two-bedroom party suites are equipped with bar, game table and large plasma TVs, and the mid-century/postmodern decor is ideal for entertaining. The Apex Suite on the seventh floor supposedly is haunted, so if you are interested in ghost hunting, request that one!

The most luxurious high-roller suites at Planet Hollywood are places I couldn't get into for more than a day, because they're usually reserved for high rollers and visiting celebrities like Arnold Schwarzenegger or Diddy. The Jonathan Adler Mega Suites have decor befitting an apartment of a billionaire bachelorette. The long silver-print-wallpapered corridor makes you feel like Alice in Wonderland upon entry. The panoramic views and modern living rooms are perfect for entertaining, and the super-large dining rooms can hold a party buffet or an extra-large sit-down dinner. Panoramic views of the Strip, red Murano glass chandeliers, surrealistic-style vases and throw pillows embroidered with the seven deadly sins help make for a fun atmosphere, with attention to detail that makes these suites some of the most attractive in Las Vegas.

Of course, the Vegas suite closest to my heart is the one I reside in at Planet Hollywood. Since I live in it it's not available for anyone else to stay

Photo shoot for Guitar World in one of the Hard Rock's best suites.

in and not marketed, but I suppose I might call it the Platinum Blonde Suite if I had to give it a name. Pamela Anderson did live in it before me, after all! I love my suite because it's huge, so when my dogs are here with me they have plenty of room to run around and play. Also, my roommate, Laura, lives in the second bedroom and my friend Claire in an adjoining suite, so it's like I have a little family right here at Planet Hollywood. The room service and proximity to Starbucks, Coffee Bean and Miracle Mile Shops are wonderfully convenient. Everyone wonders what it is like to live in a hotel; I think it's great! It reminds me a lot of living at the Playboy Mansion because of the 24-hour butler service and the constant party going on downstairs.

The decor in my room is a throwback to when the building was the Aladdin, re-built in 2000 after the last Aladdin was imploded. It's blue and yellow, part Princess Jasmine, part Marie Antoinette.

World

Vegas is the ultimate place to start over. It's also the ultimate place to create your own fantasy life — life on your own terms. Las Vegas has certainly made itself a very easy city to live in. Everything is close and convenient. People are accepting, and sometimes it seems as if anything goes.

Starting over is exactly what I did when I moved to Las Vegas. I'm still the same old Holly, but my job and lifestyle are a little different from when I lived in L.A. One thing I like about Vegas is that there are always crazy parties going on and always excuses to dress up in crazy costumes, so in that respect, it's a little like my life when I lived at the Playboy Mansion. Vegas is a place where I can do things on my own terms, though, and be independent.

When the time came for me to choose a regular cast of characters from my real-life friends for my reality show and *Girls Next Door* spin-off, *Holly's World*, Josh Strickland, my co-star in *Peepshow*, was an obvious choice. Talented, good-looking, charismatic and with a flair for the dramatic, he's perfect for television. The girls and I kind of represent the population of Vegas in a way, though I didn't consciously recognize that when I asked Angel and Laura to be part of the show.

Angel was born and raised in Las Vegas. She went to a Christian school, goes to church every Sunday, and was really unfamiliar with the Strip before she started hanging out with me. Believe it or not, that's what life seems to be like for most locals. The people who live here may or may not work on the Strip, may or may not enjoy it sometimes, but they definitely lead real lives off of it.

Laura represents the tourist. There are an average of 36.7 million of them here per year,

Vegas is the ultimate place to start over.

and they definitely make Las Vegas what it is and make most of the local jobs possible. Laura loves to socialize, party, explore, and see what the next new thing is. Her mind is focused on the present and she wouldn't mind being like one of the characters from *The Golden Girls* when she gets old.

I represent — and am — the person who comes to Vegas to start over. Las Vegas is the youngest large American city, having been founded only a little over 100 years ago. The sparse population and harsh climate of Southern Nevada made its people survivors and entrepreneurs who were always looking for a way for the city to establish itself, whether as a railroad town, agricultural center or tourist mecca.

If you have seen my show *Holly's World* on E! you will know we spend a lot of time exploring Vegas. If there is a place on the show you have seen and

(Top) The cast of *Holly's World*: Josh Strickland, Holly, Laura Croft, and Angel Porrino. (Above) Laura and Holly.

want to check out, I probably have it listed in this chapter, along with a few of my other Vegas favorites.

Holly's World Locations

Mandalay Bay: I love going to the UFC Fights; they are some of the most exciting events in Las Vegas! I like to get dressed up for them, too, like people used to for the big boxing matches in the '70s. (Unless I'm working as an octagon girl; then it's a tiny red-and-white two-piece.) The major UFC fights are always at Mandalay Bay or MGM. Personally, I like it better when they are at MGM, because I don't have to run as far to make it to my show on time after the fights.

Planet Hollywood: I live here part time, but don't try to find my suite. I'm friendly on the casino floor, not so much if someone were to randomly knock on my door. And besides, my roommate, Laura, might bite you!

Strip House at Planet Hollywood: That's where I had the conversation with my buddies about how bad the road construction in Las Vegas can get.

The Mayor's Office: City Hall is downtown at 400 Stewart Avenue, but they are building a new one, so I wouldn't count on seeing the mayor there much longer.

The Peppermill, 2985 Las Vegas Boulevard South: Our favorite hang! I love this place, especially late at night. We even spent a whole day shooting an opening for Holly's World there, but the footage ended up on the cutting-room floor. Poor Peppermill!

Pole Position Raceway, 4175 South Arville Street: This is a fun place! I had actually been there a few times before I went there on a blind date. It's a great place to have fun! Just don't bump into anyone too hard; it does hurt!

Minus Five Ice Bar: This arctic-themed bar can be found in Mandalay Place at Mandalay Bay, and

at the Monte Carlo. They have a normal bar, which kind of looks like a lodge, and then they have their ice room behind the bar area. It's in a big freezer. They provide coats and gloves for you to wear before you go inside the room made of ice. Drink from the famous "Boob Luge" and be sure to have one of my signature cocktails, the "Holly Mad-Ice-son." It's delicious!

Cashman Field, 850 Las Vegas Boulevard North: Catch a Las Vegas 51s game at Cashman Field. Who knows? It may be one of the nights they are handing out free bobbleheads!

La Perla: This is where I took Angel lingerie-shopping and told her I was buying her a boob job for her birthday. The store is in The Forum Shops at Caesars.

TAO nightclub: This is where we had The World's Biggest twenty-first Birthday Party for Angel, as well as my last birthday party. It's an amazing club, especially on Thursdays, and you will definitely have a blast there. It's in the Venetian.

Hotels Worth Exploring

Many of the Vegas casino-resorts are worth just walking into to take a look. Whether or not you get distracted by one of the gaming tables, restaurants or bars,

they are fun to explore and great places to people-watch.

Wynn Las Vegas and Encore: These are some of the prettiest casinos. I love the giant glass chandeliers, gorgeous draperies, and chairs that look like they came from a fancy retro hair salon.

Circus Circus: Across from the Wynn is Circus Circus, built in 1968. I don't think it's changed too much since then. It's bizarre in that there are live circus acts going on right above the gaming tables and a midway where you can try your luck at Skee-Ball and perhaps win a stuffed horse or a few Bob the Builder pillows, as I recently did.

The Venetian: The Venetian is absolutely beautiful with its painted ceilings, gilded columns and of course the canals with gondolas. It smells good in there, too, which is kind of apropos, as anyone who's been to the real Venice knows it could use some scenting itself. Sometimes I run into women wearing the Venetian scent, so I'm assuming they sell it somewhere.

The Mirage: The Mirage is worth seeing for its tropical rainforest atrium, 50,000-gallon saltwater aquarium behind the check-in counter and erupting volcano in the front. A valet once told me that if you ask, someone from the Mirage will take you on a tour of the under-workings of the volcano.

Imperial Palace: Against all odds, I'm fond of this old-schooler. The casino's Chinese-dragon ceiling is quaint and I love the feeling of stepping back into the '70s the minute you pull under the I.P.'s porte-cochere. They also have a cool vintage car museum. You must weave your way through this confusing labyrinth of a casino to find the museum. (Casinos are designed to be confusing, as the proprietors are hoping the customers become so dazed and confused during the search for their destination that they just plop down at a slot machine and start gambling. The I.P. is a little extra confusing, as you have to wind all the way through the casino back to this little Star Wars-era area that hasn't been updated since 1978, to the elevators that lead you to the museum.) The I.P. also has "dealertainers," blackjack dealers who double as celebrity impersonators. The last time I was there, I saw an over-the-top version of Charo and some blonde I couldn't pinpoint. My roommate, Laura, loves the Little Richard dealertainer. I highly recommend grabbing one of those huge plastic guitar drink glasses from RockHouse and stumbling your way through this Hunter S. Thompson-worthy theater of the bizarre.

The Bellagio: The Bellagio is a beautiful casino, with a Dale Chihuly blown-glass ceiling in the lobby and the Bellagio Conservatory and Gardens, which is an amazing botanical display — with free admission — that changes seasonally. There are Christmas displays, spring and summer displays and Chinese New Year displays. My favorite, however, are the fall displays. The windmills, trees with faces, humungous pumpkins and other whimsical harvest creations are delightful.

Paris Las Vegas: My favorite casino in Vegas is Paris Las Vegas, because I love the French theme. The Disney-esque French village inside the hotel is absolutely adorable. I always wish I had a condo inside one of the Parisian apartment facades they have in their little village. It all just looks so impossibly romantic! Be sure to check out the Napoleon's Dueling Piano Bar in the village section.

Planet Hollywood: There's always a lot going on in Planet Hollywood. I love that casino because of the airy, high ceilings and the gorgeous crystal-beaded columns everywhere. I also like my black-jack felts and slot machines.

The Cosmopolitan: This glamorous casino, decorated by David Rockwell, is one of my favorites. A

(Left top) View of the strip from the Mandarin Oriental. (Lower left) The amazing crystal beaded chandalier at the Cosmopolitan. (Above) The Artisan boutique hotel.

two-million bead chandalier winds itself around several stories of bars, leading up to the dining and shopping levels.

Mandarin Oriental: This is a sleek and sophisticated hotel. Take the elevator up to the bar level and you will see one of the most amazing views of the Strip, perfect to enjoy a cocktail by. Also, the gold-block walls and luxurious Asian Art Deco décor are worth seeing.

Hard Rock: If you want to people-watch and debauchery is your theme of choice, go no further than the Hard Rock. For some reason everyone gets a little crazier here. This can be a good thing or a bad thing, depending on your mood. There's also rock-n-roll memorabilia, which is fun to look at,

displayed everywhere, like KatyPerry's blue onesie and Sid Vicious's trandemark chain necklace.

Artisan: Just west of the Strip at 1501 West Sahara Avenue, this 64-room boutique hotel is surrounded by shade trees creating a stylish oasis, just minutes from all of the Vegas madness. The Harry Potter-meets-haunted mansion-meets twisted –art-gallery look of the lobby immediately transports you to another place, more mysterious and edgy than the larger-than-life style that is de rigueur in typical Vegas hotels. The main lobby is adjacent to a large bar area, which turns into an ultra-lounge at night. The pool, though small and retro compared to most Vegas mega-pools, has the secluded, sexy feel of a Hollywood hideaway, yet still has a DJ, luxury cabanas, and bottle service. Special areas for weddings at the Artisan include a miniature gothic chapel and a hidden outdoor garden area behind the pool.

The El Cortez: The El Cortez is downtown at 600 Fremont Street. It is one of my favorite casinos to walk through, as it is one of the oldest (established in 1941) and has such a storied history. The original part of the El Cortez resisted the Vegas tendency toward change and its façade remains the same in appearance as it did in the 1940s. Notorious gangster Bugsy Siegel and his associates once owned this property before getting in on the Flamingo. It is fun to take a stroll through this casino with its '70s-era super-low ceilings and glass on the doors the color of cigarette stains. Stroll up to the

Area 51 warning signs. (Left) Postcard from the El Cortez.

Las Vegas Urban Legends

I love urban legends, and Las Vegas is home to some of the craziest. Are they true or are they false? On some of them I give my opinion, but truly, we may never know . . .

Area 51: This is a patch of desert about eighty-three miles northwest of downtown Las Vegas. Shrouded in mystery, this government-owned property has become synonymous with aliens. Its location is rarely acknowledged by the government, and then only as a U.S. Air Force installation. The

Vintage Rooms and you will find at the end of the corridor a random old barbershop. I love the quirkiness of it all.

property has become synonymous with aliens. Its location is rarely acknowledged by the government, and then only as a U.S. Air Force installation. The mystery surrounding Area 51 has led people to develop several conspiracy theories regarding the place, most of them relating to extra-terrestrials.

Urban legend makes Area 51 out to be a government lab where aliens and their spacecraft are studied. Others believe it is a top-secret military-technology development site. When driving north on Las Vegas Boulevard South, as one passes McCarran International Airport, sometimes you can see a white jet with a red stripe landing or taking off. These aircraft are known as Janets and are said to shuttle workers to and from Area 51 and the Nevada Test Site. The closest you will come in Las Vegas to seeing a space alien, however, is Cosmo, the mascot of the Las Vegas 51s baseball team.

The stripper planes: If you live in Southern California and are lucky enough to know about its best-kept secret, the Bob Hope Airport in Burbank, you have probably heard about the stripper planes. Supposedly, so much money is to be made stripping in Vegas that Southern California exotic dancers find it worth the trip to fly to Vegas on the weekends. Since these girls travel every weekend, they know the Burbank airport is much less of a hassle than LAX, so no matter where they live in L.A., they will drive to Burbank. And so the Friday evening flights from Burbank to Vegas fill up with girls in track suits sporting extra-long nails, hair extensions, fake tans and loads of makeup. The stripper party plane may sound like a college boy's fantasy because of all that SoCal skin, but I have heard firsthand from more than one of my friends that this phenomenon does exist. So yes, boys, the stripper planes are real!

Suicide balconies: When I first started visiting Las Vegas, everyone told me there are no balconies in Las Vegas hotel rooms and the windows don't open because too many people were jumping to their deaths after losing all of their winnings in the casino; hotels were tired of cleaning up the mess, so they stopped building balconies.

After researching this topic, I found many other reasons balconies are undesirable. First of all, if you look at new high-rises in different cities, you will see many without balconies; a smooth glass surface can be a particularly appealing aesthetic. Second, if you look at places that do have balconies and notice all the junk that people accumulate on them, one can see how that can make the entire property look unappealing. And third, anyone who's spent more than a few days in Vegas has probably noticed what strong winds can rip through this city. Because of the winds, balconies aren't really a place Las Vegans often hang out.

Hoover Dam deaths: The massive undertaking that was the construction of Hoover Dam sparked tales of how many dead bodies are buried in the structure — allegedly workers who fell into the concrete and couldn't get out. But since the concrete sections of the dam were actually poured in very small portions, this wouldn't have been possible.

One eerie tale about the dangerous working conditions on the dam site that is true involves the last man to perish during construction. He was the son of the first man to have died on the dam project. On December 20, 1922, J.G. Tierney drowned while surveying the area, trying to find the best spot for the dam. Exactly thirteen years to the day later, his son, Patrick W. Tierney, was the last man to die working on the dam.

The Fake Roy: One day as I was getting my hair done backstage at *Peepshow*, the conversation between my hairdresser and I turned to Siegfried

> Yes, boys, the stripper planes are real!

and Roy, the most successful magic act to ever grace the Las Vegas Strip. "You know that's not the original Roy; that's his cousin," my hairdresser, Matthew, blurted out.

"What do you mean?" I asked.

Matthew went on to tell me an elaborate story about how supposedly Roy Horn died of cancer in the '80s and Siegfried, in a desperate move to save the show, tracked down a Roy look-alike — a cousin — in their native Germany. The cousin then got plastic surgery to look as much like Roy as possible and came to the States to seamlessly take Roy's place.

While Matthew insisted the story was true, and while every Vegas native seems to have heard the tale, I highly doubt its validity. I have met Siegfried and Roy numerous times and they are gracious gentleman. Meeting them wouldn't tell me anything since I didn't know them back in the day, but I just don't believe the story. In this day and age, with information everywhere, I'm sure someone from Germany who knew "Roy's cousin" would have ratted out the scheme by now.

Apparently, there was a period in the '80s when Siegfried and Roy took a break from doing their shows to go to Europe for an audience with the Pope. According to some, Roy came back looking a little different; hence the story. Instead of the usual tabloid-style plastic-surgery rumors, a wild urban legend grew that still has resident Las Vegans believing it!

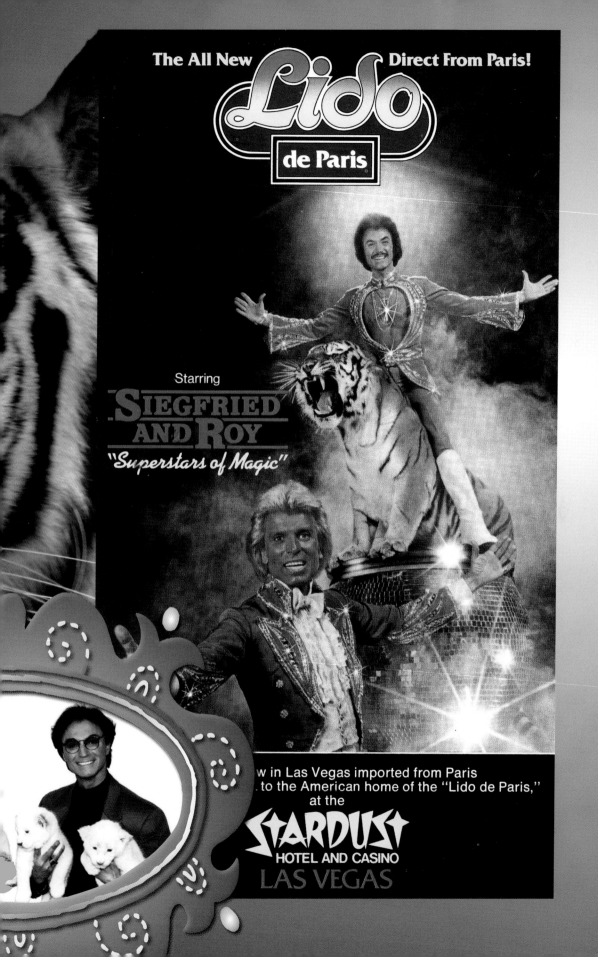

Liberace:
The Godfather Of Vegas Glam

Liberace's journey to become the icon he is today began in West Allis, Wisconsin where he was born Walter Valentino Liberace in 1919. His mother, father and siblings all were interested in and played music. It was clear from an early age that young Walter was particularly talented when it came to playing the piano, and he devoted much time to developing his skills, studying at the Wisconsin Conservatory of Music. He first performed as a soloist with the Chicago Symphony when he was twenty.

Liberace had a successful career touring the country in the '40s and '50s and played such prestigious venues as Soldier Field, the Hollywood Bowl, Carnegie Hall and Madison Square Garden. His first regular gig in Vegas was at the Riviera Hotel. He started there in 1955 as the highest-paid performer in town, making $50,000 a week — quite a lot of money in that era.

He also continued to record and tour. In the '50s and early '60s, he met the Pope and performed at the London Palladium in the first-ever-televised royal command performance.

When Liberace returned to Las Vegas in the '60s, his shows were more elaborate than ever, featuring not only his trademark candelabra atop a glittering piano and outlandish costumes, but also more theatrical staging, such as using his Rolls-Royces to make his entrances. Through the 1980s he continued to be a major draw in Las Vegas, making up to $300,000 a week.

"Mr. Showmanship," as Liberace was known, passed away in 1987 (reportedly from AIDS) in Palm Springs, California, but not until after realizing his lifelong dream of playing Radio City Music Hall. Not only did he play there, he set records for sales and attendance for his first engagement and went on to perform a record-setting twenty-one shows at the iconic venue!

Liberace's legacy lives on in many ways, one of which is the non-profit Liberace Foundation for the Performing and Creative Arts that he established in 1976. The foundation has benefitted more than 2,700 students, having awarded more than $5.8 million in scholarships and grants.

One of my favorite spots in Vegas was The Liberace Museum, which closed in 2010. The museum was established by Liberace himself in 1979 and housed many of his most elaborate possessions. It took up two whole buildings on East Tropicana Avenue, the first housing his glamorous cars — such as the mirrored Roll-Royce he used on stage — and a world-class collection of pianos, most elaborately decorated and some as old as two hundred years. The second building showcased his awards, jewelry, favorite trademark mirrored piano and out-of-this-world costumes, many of which put Lady Gaga to shame! When the museum became a drain on the foundation, supporters voted to close it, but many of the displays will live on in a traveling exhibit.

Next to the former museum site is Carluccio's Tivoli Gardens restaurant, a delicious Italian place where

Liberace used to eat, and sometimes cook. Despite having a house nearby, Liberace reportedly kept a secret apartment behind the restaurant because he loved spending late nights there so much. The restaurant features an amazing piano-shaped bar and is said to be haunted by Liberace himself.

Liberace's Las Vegas residence is privately owned. I have been lucky enough to take a tour of it and have seen that the owners lovingly preserve it so that it looks very similar to when Liberace occupied the house himself. It's at 4982 Shirley Street.

Liberace's elaborate bathtub, in his las Vegas home.

Late Night Dining

My absolute favorite Las Vegas restaurant is not a fancy place, but a quirky gem perfect for that after-nightclub-soak-up-the-alcohol snack. **The Peppermill**, located between the Riviera and a random strip mall on Las Vegas Boulevard South, is the most Las Vegas-y diner you will ever find. The diner itself looks like a Denny's collided with a roller disco, with its neon strip lights winding around plush booths. The menu is large, the portions even larger. Try the fruit plate; it's more the size of a fruit bowl, complete with whole bananas. The bread and marshmallow spread that comes with it is to die for! Behind the diner is the Peppermill's Fireside Lounge, with a water-and-fire pit straight out of the '70s.

(Left and below) Food and fun at the Peppermill.

Restaurants

On the subject of late-night haunts, **First Food and Bar** is perfect. Gourmet junk foods dominate the menu at First, which is nestled in the Shoppes at the Palazzo. I was first attracted to it by a photo of a tower of donuts served with three dipping sauces. While the desserts didn't disappoint (try the donut sundae or the homemade push-pops), the main menu is not only just as fabulously decadent, but delightfully presented — for example, the tater tots come in cute mini-fryer baskets. The sliders are delicious, as are the fish and chips and breakfast sandwiches. Be sure to try the walnut shrimp.

(Above) Gourmet junk foods from First Food and Bar at the Palazzo. (Below) Mon Ami Gabi at Paris Las Vegas. (Right) Simon at Palms Place.

My Favorite Lunch Spots

One can't-miss restaurant is **Mon Ami Gabi** at Paris Las Vegas. The bistro has a gorgeous patio right across from the Fountains at Bellagio on the Strip and also is prime seating for people-watching. The Parisian-themed meals start with a baguette and European-style butter. The chopped salad is one of my favorite salads in Las Vegas, but I also love to get breakfast foods there — even simple things like toast (extra-thick slices) and yogurt (French-style, served with fruit on top). They also offer a Bloody Mary bar on weekends for those of us who may need a little help adjusting to the new day.

The beautifully decorated **Society Café** Encore is a fabulous place for lunch. The gorgeous restaurant off the beautiful Encore casino offers my favorite mid-day meal, the box lunch. It includes an entree, such as a Kobe burger, a small chopped salad (another of my favorite salads in Las Vegas) and a couple of donut holes. I also love the tomato bisque and the lollipop chicken wings.

Another of my favorite Las Vegas restaurants is definitely **Simon**, Kerry Simon's poolside restaurant at Palms Place. They make my favorite sushi roll, the Baked California Roll, which I eat with a lot of the spicy mayo sauce on the side.

Simon is famous for Sunday brunch, with a buffet of pastries, cereals, sushi, peel-and-eat shrimp, and hot breakfast sandwiches. The pajama-clad servers can also bring you breakfast items from the menu, such as Frosted-Flake-encrusted french toast, "white trash breakfast" (including pigs in a blanket) and breakfast pizza, among many other unique selections. A Simon trademark I love is the Junk Food Platter, which comes with cotton candy, homemade caramel corn, homemade versions of Hostess treats (like the cupcake and Sno Ball), fresh-baked cookies and my favorite, Froot Loop treats, which are like Rice Krispie treats but made with the more flavorful Froot Loops! I always leave Simon way too full. Daytime meals at Simon are enhanced by the fun people-watching at the adjacent Palms Place pool. It's often pretty windy outside, so the pool looks like a mini-wave pool, making it all the more fun.

My Favorite Buffets

Buffets are everywhere in Vegas; in fact, the city is famous for them. Delicious, all-you-can-eat food at very low prices is among the attractions

The junk food platter
at Simon, Palms Place.

that lure patrons into the casinos. After the first Vegas buffet opened in the 1940s at the El Rancho Vegas (all you can eat for $1!), buffets became a Sin-City staple. Frankly, I feel there are so many great restaurant experiences here that I wouldn't recommend spending too much time in buffet lines (which are usually long on weekends; hit a buffet on a weekday, if you must). My favorite in town is **Le Village Buffet** at Paris Las Vegas, particularly around breakfast time. They have everything from Cream of Wheat to made-to-order crepes, all in a Disney-esque village-style setting, the foods divided into stations representing different areas of France.

Breakfast in a French village at Paris Las Vegas.

Junk Food Done Right

There are many "gourmet junk food" establishments in Vegas these days, but Stack definitely stands out. In the center of the Mirage, it's the perfect place to dine before two of my favorite Vegas shows, *Love* and *Terry Fator*. I took a few friends to **Stack** and they were overwhelmed at how great the selections were. This is a fun place, so don't order anything boring like a salad. Get the hot rock appetizer, steak slices you cook yourself on a large hot stone brought to your table. The appetizers are so great (my favorite in Vegas) that I recommend just ordering a whole bunch of them instead of the usual appetizer-entree routine. Try the adult tater tots and pigs in a blanket (my table of three easily went through two orders of those). Definitely save room, as the warm chocolate cake and jelly donut holes are among my favorite desserts in town.

Pizza

My favorite pizza in Vegas, whether you are visiting the restaurant or ordering delivery, is **Metro Pizza**. Metro has five locations in Las Vegas, but the Ellis Island branch on Koval Lane is conveniently located for Strip delivery.

(Below) Gourmet comfort foods at Stack at the Mirage.

Steakhouses

When I was asking around among friends regarding their favorite Vegas restaurants, one steakhouse habitually topped the list: **N9NE Steakhouse** at the Palms. This was the first quality steakhouse I ever visited where I didn't feel the need to use my favorite condiment, A-1 Steak Sauce, on my filet mignon. The steaks are absolutely delicious, but so is everything else on the menu. The Garbage Salad is great, and don't leave without trying the lobster mashed potatoes. Campfire S'mores are a great dessert — served with your own mini-campfire in a can, marshmallows, chocolate-covered graham crackers, and chocolate ice cream. Espresso shots from the bar are tasty, and a great way to help keep alert for a fun night ahead!

Usually, each casino-resort has a sushi place and a steakhouse.

Celebrity-chef establishments have peppered the Strip since the '90s, but before they were a must-have for every property, the popular nice restaurant to take visiting friends, according to some trusty locals, was **The Steakhouse at Circus Circus**. Cozy and quaint compared to the more trendy places now common in Las Vegas, the restaurant's green-and-burgundy brass-rail decor — complete with paintings of cattle — feels very Main Street USA. The food is not only delicious, but each steak dinner is served with a soup or salad and two sides, unlike the more modern steakhouses, where the sides are a la carte. The desserts are yummy, too, and come with a side of hot fudge, clown-sugar sprinkles and whipped cream.

Certainly the steakhouse with the sexiest atmosphere is **Strip House** at Planet Hollywood. Retro bordello-style red-flocked wallpaper and vintage burlesque photographs cover the walls of the romantic, dimly lit restaurant. In addition to outstanding entrees like ahi tuna, Strip House serves some of my favorite appetizers, such as an organic green salad served in a Parmesan shell and lobster bisque. Last but not

(Left) The Steakhouse at Circus Circus = meat meat and more more.

least is one of my favorite desserts in all of Vegas, the twenty-five-layer chocolate cake!

One of my favorite restaurants in Los Angeles is Mastro's in Beverly Hills, so I was thrilled when the opening of CityCenter not long after my move to Las Vegas brought a **Mastro's Ocean Club** to Crystals, CityCenter's shopping mall. I even prefer this Mastro's to the Los Angeles one, first and foremost due to the quirky architecture. The restaurant's seating spills out into a space-age tree-house-like structure that stands in the middle of the sleek, eco-futuristic shopping center. It's fun sitting in the pod. Shrimp cocktails are served on dry ice, as is the signature Mastro's Martini, giving them a witch's-brew look. Usually I am so stuffed after my dinner at Mastro's that I don't order dessert, but after a bite of a friend's Warm Butter Cake I quickly changed my tune. It is so good and it melts in your mouth!

Union in Aria at CityCenter is right off the casino floor, in an enchanted forest of arching wood structures. The impeccable service and delicious menu will have you feeling right at home in the wonderland created by architect Adam Tihany. The seafood tower (served with dry ice), roasted tomato soup with bacon-tomato grilled-cheese mini-sandwich, sliders, "all-year" corn, and mac and cheese are my favorite appetizers and sides. Finish it off with one of their homemade lollipops!

The Golden Steer is the most old-school of the Vegas steakhouses, and is in fact the second-oldest restaurant in the city (the oldest being El Sombrero Café, established in 1950). Opened in 1958, the Golden Steer is in an unassuming strip mall just off the Strip on Sahara Avenue, right next to Bonanza Gifts, also known as the World's Largest Souvenir Shop. Though the restaurant has been expanded since 1958, the original booths remain and are dedicated to famous patrons past and present. Plaques above the booths read "Elvis Presley," "Frank Sinatra," "Sammy Davis Jr.," "Mario Andretti" and many more. Besides their "best steaks on earth

(Below) "The pod" at Mastro's Ocean Club. (Right) Cupcakes at Union.

since 1958," the Golden Steer offers a wide variety of seafood, Italian dishes, salads and appetizers, my favorite of which are the large, seafood-stuffed mushroom caps. The staff includes many people who have been with the restaurant for more than thirty years and can tell you the whole history of the place, as the lovely hostess told me the first time I visited. You will want to see "the mob room," the secret, hidden dining room next to Mayor Oscar Goodman's booth, where the mob allegedly ate in secret. Finish your dining experience with the outstanding Cherries Jubilee dessert, which is flambéed tableside.

Amazing Views

The first Las Vegas restaurant I dined in was **VooDoo Steak**, way back in 2001. I don't even remember what I had to eat; I just remember being impressed with the amazing views from atop the fifty-one-story Rio after a ride up a glass elevator on the side of the building. I was equally impressed with the extensive drink menu featuring all kinds of exotic, sweet concoctions, the most popular of which seemed to be the Witch's Brew, a fruity punch served in a large glass with multiple straws and dry ice, making the drink foam like a witchy cauldron.

Two other restaurant experiences with amazing, romantic views are **The Eiffel Tower** restaurant at Paris Las Vegas and **Top of The World** at the Stratosphere. The food at both is delicious, the view from the rotating restaurant atop The Stratosphere is more impressive, but the Eiffel Tower is much easier to get to and more stylishly decorated. Either restaurant is perfect for a romantic, memorable evening.

One of my favorite views in Vegas is not of the city lights, but of the Lake of Dreams at The Wynn, the three-acre lake and waterfall built as an

(Below) Dining area with glass kitchen in the background at Lakeside Grill located inside Wynn hotel-casino.

attraction which, unlike the Mirage volcano and Bellagio fountains, must be viewed from inside its host resort. The waterfall provides a screen for projections, kind of like a drive-in movie screen, and a giant, animatronic frog climbs atop the fall to "sing along" to selected songs at regular intervals. Great views of the Lake can be had from SW Steakhouse and Lakeside Grill. Lakeside serves American dishes and SW is the acclaimed steakhouse at the Wynn.

Asian

My favorite sushi spot in the city is **Koi** at Planet Hollywood; I eat there

A puppet frog at the Lake of Dreams at Wynn Las Vegas hotel-casino, sings Garth Brooks' "Friends in Low Places."

several times a week. Roomier and less scene-y than its L.A. counterpart, the Vegas Koi is just as delicious and has a beautiful view of the Strip and sleek, modern decor. When it's still daylight, I like to sit in the Fountain Room, named for its Strip view facing the Bellagio fountains. It's a great spot to people-watch as Strip tourists stroll the sidewalks below. I can't get enough of the tiger rolls, dragon rolls and California rolls, and I also love the rock shrimp served over California rolls.

For late night sushi, I would recommend **Kaizen Fusion Roll and Sushi** on Paradise across from the Hard Rock. Serving Japanese and Korean dishes, this spot is a favorite late night restaurant of many of

my friends. Kaizen is open from 5:30 p.m. to 4 a.m. Sundays through Thursdays and from 5:30 p.m. to 6 a.m. Fridays and Saturdays.

Tao at the Venetian is a great place to eat dinner, whether or not you plan on partying at their world-famous club afterward. One of Tao's standout dishes is Chilean sea bass served on a stick, covered in a delicious sauce. I also love the mochi, with coconut my favorite flavor. The white coconut ice cream is surrounded by brown coconut-flavored dough, so the mochi looks like a little coconut when you bite into it.

The sumptuously decorated **Jasmine** at the Bellagio makes an impression before you even get your food, not just with its gorgeous decor and Versace butterfly-garden china, but also with the amazing view. Jasmine is one of a handful of restaurants sprinkled along the man-made Strip-side lake at

(Above left and right) Tao at the Venetian.
(Far right) Jasmine at Bellagio.

the Lake Como-themed resort, where the dancing fountains go off every half-hour. It's difficult for me to peel my eyes away from my surroundings long enough to look at the menu, but the Hong Kong/Cantonese fare is certainly worth it. My favorite entree is the sweet-and-sour pork served in a pineapple.

Buried deep inside the Gold Coast Casino is a more affordable Chinese food option, the local favorite, **Ping Pang Pong**, consistently voted "Best Dim Sum" in town. Ping Pang Pong serves dim sum brunch from 10 a.m. to 3 p.m. daily and dinner selections from 5 p.m. to 3 a.m. one can enjoy dinner selections in the evening through late night. My favorite dishes are the pot stickers and the sesame shrimp rolls.

You may have a **Benihana** in your hometown, but the one at the Las Vegas Hilton, just east of the Strip, is extra-special on a grand Vegas scale. Entry is through a two-story indoor Japanese garden with thunder, lighting, rainfall, and fireworks effects in the faux sky.

German

Having visited and loved the Hofbrauhaus in Munich, I was eager to check out the replica a few blocks off the Strip in Las Vegas. Near the Hard Rock on Paradise Road and Harmon Avenue, the **Hofbrauhaus** has live music nightly, imported German beer, and a traditional menu. It also has a beer garden that's modeled after the original in Munich but actually is indoors, with trees and cloud-painted ceilings. The huge, soft pretzels are amazing and come with two types of mustard and a German cheese spread called obatzer. My other favorite items include the potato soup and pickles. I get so full of those that I don't even usually order an entree, but I always get dessert; the plum or apricot strudel is outstanding. If you are with a large group, get the dessert tower so you can sample everything. Oktoberfest is a special time at Hofbrauhaus Las Vegas, with local celebrities tapping the keg to much fanfare every week in October.

Italian

I absolutely love Italian food. One of the first places I think of when I think of places that definitely get it right is **Battista's Hole in the Wall** on Flamingo Road, right behind the Flamingo. Battista's is delightfully old school and terribly cluttered, kind of like the original version of what a Buca di Beppo tries to look like. I particularly enjoy perusing their collection of miniature liquor bottles on display in the front of the restaurant. There also are vintage souvenir decanters from casinos of yore, such as the Stardust and the Hacienda, the likes of which I can't even find on eBay. A delicious Italian meal, complete with decanters of wine automatically brought to the table, can be enjoyed while listening to the musical skills of Gordy, their resident accordionist.

Another old-school Italian favorite is **Piero's** at 355 Convention Center Drive, which serves my favorite pasta dishes in town. I was originally attracted to it because scenes in one of my favorite movies, *Casino*, were shot there. Upon visiting I quickly fell in love with

the food, particularly the Fettuccini a Modo Mio. I also love the avocado and hearts of palm salad.

The excellent Mob-themed restaurant, **Capo's**, at 5675 W. Sahara Avenue, serves up not only great Italian food but also amazing atmosphere with their speakeasy-like entryway, dark, flocked wallpaper, piano, and cozy booths. The spinach-cheese ravioli is a personal favorite.

Lavo is a restaurant and nightclub where I have hosted many fun events, and my buddies and I love to indulge in the delicious family-style dishes. I don't usually like meatballs, but those from Lavo are an exception. Some of our other favorites include Kobe-stuffed rice balls and crispy calamari, and the fried Oreos are a can't-miss for dessert!

I've tried to stay away from recommending chain restaurants in this book, not because I don't enjoy them like everyone else but because a trip to Vegas calls for taking advantage of things you wouldn't find at home. One of the few exceptions I have to mention is **Buca Di Beppo**, simply because I am there so often that it would be strange not to. The pizza with pepperoni and pepperoncinis is so tasty that I crave it all the time. I always go to the location at 412 West Flamingo Road, because it's near the Strip. I love all the wacky décor and notice something new every time I go! I love sitting in The Pope's Room, which has a huge round table with a kind-of-creepy bust of a Pope staring at you from under glass in the center. Just remember to share the portions with a friend. Everything is served family style and the servings are huge!

Getting into it at Buca di Beppo.

Mexican

There's a tie for my favorite chips and salsa in Las Vegas, between **Dona Maria's** near Las Vegas and Charleston boulevards downtown (they also have the best tamales) and **T&T** (Tacos and Tequila) at the Luxor. I could live on T&T's chips and green salsa, though their red salsa is really good, too. Under an abstract metal sombrero on the Luxor's atrium level, T&T is a lively spot with photo booth, mariachi Sunday brunches, and cute waitresses in cutoff shorts. I love that it's open from 11 a.m. to 11 p.m., so it's great for dinner or for brunch; you know you crave some good Mexican food after a long night of drinking! Try one of their delicious strawberry agave margaritas as a hair-of-the-dog hangover cure. My favorite dish there is a veggie, black bean and cheese burrito with green sauce on top. It's not on the menu, but they make it for me anyway and it's delicious! I'm convinced it's healthy, too, because I pigged out on their chips, salsa, and burritos every morning for months on end and never gained weight.

Dos Caminos is famous for its guacamole, and for good reason. Don't fill up on it, though, or you will miss their amazing entrees, of which my favorite is the open-faced grilled-shrimp quesadilla. The first Dos Caminos outside New York City, the restaurant and bar is located right off the casino floor in The Palazzo.

Knowing there had to be some good Mexican food off the Strip, I asked a trusty pal about it and he recommended **Casa Don Juan** on Main Street downtown. I was immediately fond of the place, as the kitschy Mexican decor, staff uniforms and family-owned, down-home vibe reminded me of my favorite little Mexican places in L.A., El Coyote and El Compadre's. I like to order the flautas appetizer to share with a friend, and I particularly like their homemade rainbow cake for dessert.

(Left and below) Flautas and Rainbow Cake at Casa Don Juan.

The Best Places for a Business Lunch

The seems-calm-even-when-packed **Verandah** is the perfect place for an upscale business lunch. At the Four Seasons at Mandalay Bay, the Verandah has indoor and outdoor seating and a mellow vibe not often found on the Strip. I love the iced tea, because the ice cubes are made of the same tea you are drinking, so melting ice doesn't dilute your drink. More restaurants should catch on to this idea! A delicious selection of salads, pizzas, sandwiches, and soups in addition to signature dishes make this one of my favorite places to meet and eat.

(Above) MOzen bistro, and its Mandarin Oriental Bento.

Located in the Mandarin Oriental and with fabulous views of the Strip and CityCenter, **MOzen Bistro** is a great business-casual spot to try a tasty variety of Asian and American dishes. Sushi rolls and sashimi always are favorites of mine, as is the Mandarin Oriental Bento, which offers a new surprise each day with a variety of tapas and small plates. I also love the 24-hour pulled-pork barbecue sandwich.

The Mood Restaurant at the Artisan is a favorite of mine, not only for their awesome food (try the lobster BLT), but for the ambience on the patio, which is surrounded by shade trees — perfect for a sunny day.

Sweets and Treats

Sugar Factory: *There are Sugar Factories in the Mirage, Planet Hollywood and Paris Las Vegas. Not only do they have the best selection of candies (my favorite are the chocolate gummy bears), but also the Planet Hollywood location has the best milkshakes EVER! Try the Birthday Cake or the Blueberry Pancake flavors. The red-velvet brownies also are to die for.*

Beso: *This popular restaurant in Crystal's at City-Center has one of my favorite desserts: churros! These churros are so soft and amazing. They come with delicious chocolate and caramel dipping sauces.*

Red Velvet Cafe: *This fabulous vegan restaurant is west of the Strip at 7875 West Sahara Avenue and it's definitely worth tracking down! Their red velvet cake is surprisingly low-calorie and the best I've ever tasted. The same can be said for their chocolate chip cookies. I always buy a packet to go!*

The Cupcakery: *I love this place for the delicious variety of cupcakes. Some of my favorites are the Grasshopper (chocolate mint), Boston Dream and El Rolo. Also, the cupcakes are relatively small, so you can eat one without feeling too guilty. They also make a Trip to Graceland cupcake, which is an Elvis-inspired peanut-butter-banana-and-bacon concoction! There are Cupcakery stores in The Monte Carlo and at 9690 S. Eastern Avenue and 7175 W. Lake Mead Boulevard.*

Pamplemousse, 400 E. Sahara Ave.: *The Grand Marnier Souffle is one of my favorite desserts in town.*

The Pirate's Chest Sundae at Serendipity 3 is big enough to share with a whole table full of friends! I especially love the heaping servings of cheesecake and peanut butter fluff piled on top of the sundae.

It's difficult to describe — just delicious and totally different from anything else I have tried. Pamplemousse has been around since the '70s and the building was converted from a home to a restaurant, so it has a quaint French-country cottage feel to it. It's a romantic, out-of-the-way little place, a perfect spot to take a date somewhere quiet off the Strip.

*   **Serendipity 3:** At Caesars Palace, it's a great place for a salad, burger, and of course, a Frrrozen Hot Chocolate!*

115

Vegas V

The Evolution of the

ixens: Showgirl

The showgirl is without a doubt one of the most recognizable symbols of Las Vegas. Her ubiquitousness stems from the Vegas tendency for every resort to try to outdo each other; one gets a good thing going and countless imitators pop up immediately, trying to one-up their competitors in search of the tourist dollar.

Pretty girls have been one of Vegas' major attractions since the early days, first popping up as stage dressing, then as Ziegfeld-girl-type models, and exotic Parisian imports. The modern version is simpler and sexier — although the traditional heavy-headdress-laden model can still be found in Donn Arden's thirty-years-running *Jubilee!* at Bally's or on the arm of Mayor Oscar Goodman almost anytime he is making a public appearance.

The Las Vegas showgirl traces her roots to 19th-century Paris and the *Folies Bergere*. Though it certainly wasn't the first establishment to employ a scantily clad stage seductress or two to draw a crowd, the *Folies Bergere* could be considered the gestation ground for all showgirls that followed. Established in 1869, it was — and still is — an opera house featuring live entertainment and beautiful, scantily clad women. Josephine Baker became a sensation in Paris upon the debut of her act in a skimpy banana skirt at the *Folies*.

The popularity of the *Folies Bergere* inspired the *Ziegfeld Follies*, extravagant Broadway spectacles staged by impresario Florenz Ziegfeld from 1907 through 1931. Though the *Follies* featured a variety of talented entertainers, they are most remembered for their beautiful women, Ziegfeld's famous "Follies Girls." On a mission to "glorify the American girl," Ziegfeld had his women draped in the most elaborate showy costumes, sometimes in varying states of nudity. He was able to get away with this on Broadway in the early 20th century by having the semi-nude women motionless on stage, posed in a tableau as if depicting a work of art.

By the mid-20th century the vaudeville and burlesque circuit, offering a variety of live entertainment, was falling out of favor in America because of the rising popularity of television. At around the same time, luxury resorts were popping up along what would become the Las Vegas Strip, and they were hungry to book top-notch entertainment to attract customers. Every place on

(Left) A *Ziegfeld Follies* girl; (Above) the 1945 film
Ziegfeld Follies' representation of the stage show.

the Strip had showgirls, often dressed in cutesy costumes reflecting the resorts' themes — pink for the Flamingo's dancers and Western saloon-girl wear at The Last Frontier, for example. The women danced on stage between the acts booked into the showroom.

Taking the showgirl to another level was Jack Entratter, who came to Las Vegas from the posh world of New York nightclubs. He was part-owner of the famous Copacabana Club in New York, where he had established the chorus line, selecting the dancers and dubbing them the Copa Girls. When Entratter came to the newly built Sands as entertainment director in 1952, he brought the Copa Girls concept with him. What bested the other dance troupes on the Strip was Entratter's eye for beauty. He didn't care whether a Copa Girl could dance, but he had very strict physical requirements: 5 feet, 4 inches tall; 116 pounds; roughly 32–24–34 measurements; small features; and an oval face. The Copa Girls also were used in publicity stunts and photos to promote the Sands. He costumed the girls elaborately and showcased them in the style of the *Ziegfeld Follies*, more model-on-stage than actual dancer. The Sands even put on a new version of the *Ziegfeld Follies*, featuring Frank Sinatra, in 1954.

One thing that differentiated the Copa Girls is that the showgirls at the Sands were never undressed, even after topless shows became the trend on the Strip in the late '50s.

(Above) "Dice Number" George Moro girls at the El Rancho in the 1950s. (Below) Frank Sinatra and the Copa Girls at the Sands, about 1954. (Bottom) Betty Bunch, one of the first Vegas showgirls.

According to Steve Fischer's *When The Mob Ran Vegas*, a curvy brunette named Lisa Melford Malouf was the first nude showgirl on the Strip, when in 1957 she posed tableau-style, standing still on stage at the Riviera.

The first show to incorporate toplessness regularly on the Strip was *Minksy's Follies* at The Dunes. The nudity was controversial, but after it opened in 1957, set an attendance record of 16,000 in one week and saved the Dunes from financial ruin, it was clear that the topless show was here to stay.

Adding their own brand of glamour to the Las Vegas Strip were sexy headliners such as Lili St. Cyr, Jayne Mansfield and Ann-Margret. St. Cyr was born Willis Marie Van Schaack in Minneapolis. Growing into a stunning, statuesque blonde, Lili, along with her sister, found work as a chorus dancer at the Florentine Gardens in Hollywood. This gig would set her on the path to becoming the queen of striptease burlesque in the 1950s. Ambition, creativity, and attention to detail and quality made Lili an excellent show woman who became a sensation performing solo striptease numbers in the hottest nightclubs in Hollywood and around the world.

One of Lili's residencies included a six-week-a-year contract with the El Rancho Vegas, the first resort on the Las Vegas Strip. The proprietors of the El Rancho worked with her to develop what would become one of her signature routines, which was performed suspended over the audience in a human-sized birdcage. At first, she balked at the idea because of a fear of heights, but after being plied with jewelry, a silver-fox fur, and a newly redecorated hotel suite, she confronted her fear and went forward with the cage routine.

(Top, above) Lili St. Cyr.

Despite a disastrous first night (Lili was knocked unconscious when the cage hit her in the head during her dismount), she turned the act into one of her signatures, delighting audiences

as articles of her clothing fell on their heads twice nightly, seven times a week.

During this time, Lili St. Cyr was promoted as "The Most Fabulous Girl in the World" and "The Anatomic Bomb," a reference to atomic tests that were going on nearby in the '50s. She married one of her numerous husbands, actor Ted Jordan, at the El Rancho Vegas. After the resort burned down in 1960, she returned to Vegas to perform several times throughout her life. Though she headlined at the Dunes, the Silver Slipper, the Castaways, and the Aladdin, Lili made clear in her autobiography, *Ma Vie de Stripteaseuse*, that her fondest memories of Las Vegas were from her days at the El Rancho.

Another blonde headliner who made quite the impression on Las Vegas was movie star Jayne Mansfield. Often thought of as the "runner-up" of sorts to Marilyn Monroe, Mansfield pushed the voluptuous pin-up image to its limits through her tireless ambition and shrewd eye for publicity. After two hit movies, Mansfield headlined at the Tropicana in *Tropicana Holiday* in 1958 and returned the following year to star in *French Dressing*. Vegas resorts were willing to pay stars huge sums of money to entertain

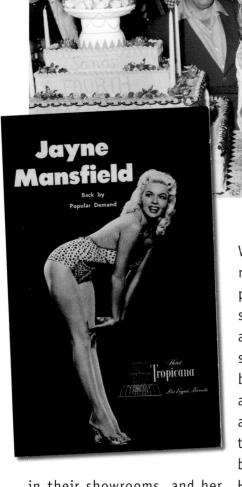

Jayne Mansfield

Back by Popular Demand

Hotel Tropicana
Las Vegas, Nevada

Ann-Margret's debut in Las Vegas was as an unknown nineteen-year-old in 1960 as part of George Burns' Christmas show at the Sahara. Her talent and charm as showcased in Burns' show landed her no less than a booking on the *Jack Benny Show*, a role in the movie *State Fair*, and a recording contract with RCA. After becoming a major Hollywood star and sex symbol, she returned to Vegas in 1967 to perform in her own show at the Riviera. Elvis Presley and George Burns showed up on opening night to lend their support.

Ann-Margret continued to play Vegas in new productions built around her through the '70s and '80s, becoming one of

in their showrooms, and her Vegas engagements paid for the construction of her "Pink Palace" in Beverly Hills, complete with heart-shaped swimming pool.

One of the movies' most Vegas-y vixens, Ann-Margret, would have a lucrative career performing consistently on the Vegas Strip for more than forty years. As the female lead in Elvis Presley's *Viva Las Vegas*, she perfectly embodied the beautiful, sexy singer-dancer ideal for the Strip.

the city's highest-paid entertainers of the time. She continued performing live (and looking fabulous) in Vegas into her 50s!

The most elaborate and first true spectacular to land on the Las Vegas Strip was the long-running *Lido de Paris* at the Stardust hotel and casino. *Lido* was significant in Vegas showgirl history in many ways — specifically because it was the first spectacle imported directly from Paris, the first large production produced by Donn Arden (who could be considered the father of the classic Vegas showgirl) and introduced the elaborate, custom-built stage to the Strip spectacle.

When the Stardust was preparing to open in the late '50s, it brought *Lido* from Paris to the hotel's Continental showroom, which had been built with special hydraulic stage lifts for the elaborate set changes required. The sets included an ice-skating rink and a swimming pool! When the spectacular opened with the Stardust in 1958, it immediately became a must-see Vegas sensation, drawing numerous guests to the property and setting off a wave of imitators up and down the Strip.

The *Lido's* showgirls were topless, and the fact that the show and the dancers themselves came directly from France and were supported by top-caliber production values made the nudity appear artistic, Continental — and acceptable in the eyes of the 1950s American tourist. Without this element of sophistication and beauty, the topless trend on the Las Vegas Strip may not have survived conservative scrutiny.

Lido evolved every year and a half or so, new routines developing around the amazing effects, keeping the show fresh so returning Stardust guests would want to see it again and again.

And the statuesque, leggy, headdress-wearing, rhinestone-bedecked showgirl who became synonymous with Las Vegas had made her debut. The

(Above) *Hallalujah, Hollywood!*

124

(Below) *Jubilee!*

previously reigning Strip showgirls, the Copa Girls, were pretty but of average height and simply modeled the elaborate costumes. The *Lido* girls were handpicked by Arden and his longtime associate. Margaret "Miss Bluebell" Kelly, and the Bluebell Girls were always tall, long-legged, classically trained dancers. With long necks to show off the elaborate headdresses and pleasant demeanors to project an aura of true enjoyment of the stage, the Bluebell Girl image came to represent the top echelon in the Vegas showgirl world. This look can still be seen in Bally's *Jubilee!*, the last remaining Donn Arden spectacular on the Strip.

Arriving from Paris on the heels of *Lido* was *Folies Bergere*, a replica of the Parisian show by the same name. It found a home — and a fifty year-run! — at the Tropicana, which opened on the southernmost end of the Strip in 1958.

Folies holds the record as the longest-running show on the Strip. In fact, the grandmother of my roommate, Laura, saw the show the year it opened and it made such an impression on her that she traveled to Vegas in 2009 specifically to see the show again on hearing of its impending close. *Folies* was a French-music-hall-themed variety show, featuring traditional Parisian showgirls and a spectacular can-can closing number.

Folies also is notable for the fact that Siegfried and Roy got their start there as one of the novelty acts. With their repertoire of illusions and big cats, Siegfried and Roy went on to many other Strip venues, eventually ending up as The Mirage's main show for a thirteen-year run. Lance Burton also got his Vegas start in *Folies*, going on to headline his own highly successful shows at the Hacienda and the Monte Carlo.

The third major player in the Parisian-showgirl-spectacular craze on the Strip was *Casino de Paris* at The Dunes. Replacing *Minsky's Follies*, Casino lasted from 1963 through the '80s and featured a stage that moved out into the audience.

Indicative of the popularity of showgirl entertainment at the time, there was room for more than one of these shows at some resorts. The Dunes, for example, not only had *Casino de Paris* but also *Vive Les Girls*, in a smaller theater on a smaller stage.

As Vegas moved into the '70s, larger resorts with more and more hotel rooms were sprouting up, such as Kirk Kerkorian's International Hotel and his MGM Grand. Befitting the hotel with the most rooms in the world at the time, the MGM Grand had the showroom with the world's largest stage and largest backstage area. Dubbed the Ziegfeld Room, the showroom was home to another Donn Arden spectacle, this one with the Vegas showgirl in Hollywood-themed numbers, straight out of the Busby Berkeley musicals of Hollywood's golden age. The costumes of *Hallelujah Hollywood!*, designed by the legendary Bob Mackie and Ray Aghayan, were the utmost in extravagance. The show featured a grand total of 700 costumes! After a six-year run, *Hallelujah Hollywood!* closed in favor of a new Donn Arden spectacle, *Jubilee!* The lavish stage production still plays at the same location, which is now Bally's. For the visitor who wants to take a trip back in time and see an old-school Vegas spectacular, *Jubilee!* is just as it was when it opened in 1980, with showgirls, dancers, showboys, elaborate costumes, and unbelievable sets. *Jubilee!* Is the last remaining classic Vegas showgirl show.

Through the '80s, in addition to mainstays like *Jubilee!*, *Lido*, and *Folies Bergere*, more showgirl spectacles were added to the tourism corridor, such as *City Lites* at the Hilton, *Sizzle* at the Sands, and *Splash* at the Riviera, the latter a variety show featuring a large water tank for dancers to plunge into. *Ice Fantasy* at the Hacienda and *Razzle-Dazzle* at the Flamingo showcased showgirls on ice skates.

This photo promoting the Hacienda's *Ice Fantasy* was so popular, it was stolen off of taxicabs (model: Tracey Vaccaro).

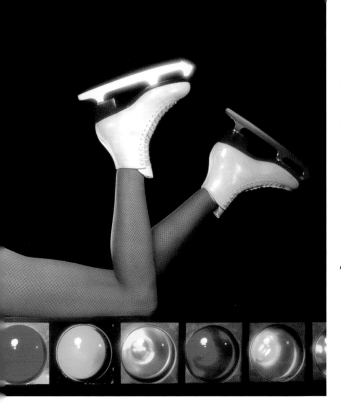

(Below left) *Crazy Girls* at the Riviera. (Right) Aki descends the stairs in *Enter The Night*.

Since the topless showgirl seemed almost quaint by the 1980s, racier shows were finding their way onto the Strip, such as *Crazy Girls* at the Riviera, a knock-off of Paris' *Crazy Horse*, featuring extremely similar numbers, but with less production value and polish. *Crazy Girls* still is going strong at the Riviera, and its advertisement has become a campy bit of Vegas iconography, famous among locals and tourists for its thong-clad models, Motley-Crue-worthy '80s hair and the slogan, "No Ifs, Ands, or Butts!"

The '90s ushered in the popularity of strip clubs as the female eye-candy entertainment of choice. The traditional shows on the Strip suffered, as resorts could no longer justify the extravagant costs of such spectacles, with audiences lured away by Cirque du Soleil's $100-million spectaculars. *Lido* closed in 1991 after a thirty-two-year run. It was replaced by *Enter The Night*, which attempted to update showgirls "for the new millennium" with contemporary music and real singing. The show lasted until 1999. The movie *Showgirls*, starring Elizabeth Berkley as a runaway stripper trying to make it in the fictional *Goddess* at the Stardust, didn't do much for the showgirl image, portraying the industry as exceedingly seedy. And with acting so bad, the drama turned into an unwitting cult comedy classic.

New shows that opened during this era were smaller in scale, such as *Showgirls* at the Rio and the magician/showgirl hybrid *Showgirls of Magic* at the San Remo.

Taking a move from the 1950s Vegas-entertainment-director playbook, the MGM Grand imported a Parisian girlie show from France, this time on a smaller, less expensive scale than the *Lidos* and *Folies Bergeres* of old. The Crazy Horse Saloon in Paris has a longstanding tradition of gorgeous, talented dancers portrayed in artistic numbers using projected light patterns on the women's skin. The intimate theater, small stage, and artistic showcasing of the women's bodies leave no room for the massive headdresses and showgirl costumery of old.

The neo-burlesque trend swept through Vegas in the early 2000s. In an effort by the casino-resorts to keep customers on property and not lured away to strip clubs, various properties experimented with having "burlesque" striptease shows on their properties. Because law prohibits strip clubs in gaming establishments, the burlesque entertainment was never nude, but down to pasties and G-string at Forty Deuce at Mandalay Bay. The old-school duplicate of the L.A. hotspot had competition from Tangerine, a nightclub at Treasure Island that featured burlesque dancers in the club. A Pussycat Dolls Lounge was adjacent to Pure nightclub in Caesars Palace.

The trend didn't last through 2010, as the burlesque performances weren't the experience a strip-club-bound guy was looking for.

Despite the fact that the showgirl spectacular no longer dominates the Strip, beautiful and talented dancers still are found all over Vegas.

The showgirl will always be a Vegas icon, whether onstage at the classic *Jubilee!*, on the arm of the mayor, or reinvented in the newest shows in Las Vegas.

(Above) Mayor Oscar Goodman takes his showgirls on all his official outings. (Left) Backstage at Crazy Horse Paris with headliner, Claire Sinclair. (Right) I would never have made it as a Jubilee! girl — I'm too short!

Chapter Seven

Glitter
Downtown Las Vegas

One of my favorite things is to take a mini-vacation in downtown Las Vegas. Just a few minutes north of the Strip, the original part of town holds many fun treasures.

My favorite place to stay is the Golden Nugget. Right on Fremont Street, the Nugget commonly is regarded as the most luxurious hotel downtown, as well as one of the most historic. It was opened in 1946 by an ex-Los Angeles vice detective and initially marketed as the largest casino in the world. When Steve Wynn took over in the '70s, the property underwent a massive renovation. It soon became home to Frank Sinatra, who was paid $10 million to perform there for three years. The Nugget was renovated again in 2005 and is the site of some of my Vegas favorites.

My favorite pool in Las Vegas is definitely the Nugget's Tank, named for its shark-tank centerpiece. The Tank is home to five species of shark — sandtiger, nurse, Pacific blacktip, zebra and brown — as well as stingray, and game fish. What makes the pool extra-exciting is the three-story waterslide that runs through the middle of the shark tank.

The sides of the slide are clear in the tank, so if you can keep your eyes open during the exhilarating plunge, you can enjoy a 360-degree view of sharks and other marine life swimming around

Gulch:

GLITTER GULCH

you. It's definitely a unique experience and one you will want to do again and again!

My favorite clothing store downtown is the Nugget's Style and Trend, which carries some of my favorite casual brands like Juicy Couture and Nick and Mo, as well as lots of cute jewelry. It's the perfect place to find comfortable and stylish vacation-wear if you didn't pack enough for your trip.

Every major hotel/casino has an affordable cafe that serves diner-style food, and many look about as attractive as a greasy spoon. The Carson Street Cafe at the Nugget is nicer than most, with the type of decor usually reserved for the more expensive restaurants. Ask for my favorite waitress, Laura; she's a hoot!

On one of my first trips to Vegas I wanted to walk through all of the casinos and just check out the atmosphere — see the different types of games, themed decor, and what people were up to. I did this with a group of friends before my friend Ashley's wedding. We tried doing this on the Strip, which was a VERY long walk, to say the least. We tried using the monorail system, which doesn't span more than a few resorts at a time. We took cabs and we walked. A block on the Strip is a LOOOOOOONG block. As you will discover, that Excalibur castle may look nearby, but after walking a half-hour or so, you still aren't there.

If you want to stroll through a few casinos in a short time, I suggest doing it on Fremont Street instead. You can see many different casinos in an

afternoon because they are all right next to each other and line Fremont Street, which is closed off to most traffic and shaded by the Fremont Street Experience canopy. At night, the underside of the canopy lights up, displaying the world's largest light show. The lights and sounds of the Fremont Street Experience sometimes prompt people to lie down in the middle of the street to enjoy the show, which is an amusing sight.

The downtown casinos are generally older than the ones on the Strip, and collectively more downscale, but I think that makes them a little more fun to explore. The casino floors always seem to be more packed with gamblers — especially those with a glazed look of resigned desperation on their faces, which is definitely worth observing.

The Golden Nugget is the most plush, complete with gorgeous blown-glass chandeliers and a display showcasing the world's largest golden nugget, the 61-pound "Hand of Faith."

Across Casino Center Boulevard is the Four Queens. Inside this casino that looks like a

Victorian railroad station is one of my favorite restaurants, **Hugo's Cellar**. It is open only for dinner, and definitely worth a reservation. The old-school, romantic, speakeasy-cellar-style spot would have been the perfect place for a prom dinner if you could have afforded it back then. Women are given roses upon entrance and the restaurant is a dimly lit hideaway that feels far from any casino atmosphere. The side-table salad is made for you and in front of you, and you pick the ingredients. The fruit sorbet on mini-ice cream cones and chocolate-dipped strawberries served with every meal also are fabulous. I highly recommend the hot-rock specialty appetizer, in which sizzling slabs of granite are brought to the table with chicken, shrimp, swordfish, and filet mignon to cook on top, along with several dipping sauces.

Next to the Four Queens is Fitzgeralds, the Irish-themed casino sitting under a neon rainbow and pot of gold. My favorite spot to people-watch on Fremont Street is from the casino-hotel's Krispy Kreme Donuts patio (this is a vacation, remember;

no better time to indulge in delicious donuts). No alcoholic drinks are allowed on the patio, but watching drunk people is so much more fun when you are sober, anyway.

Head across the street to the Fremont and then on to Binion's, a Western-themed casino where you can take your photo with the $1 million they have on display.

My favorite place to grab a drink on Fremont Street is La Bayou. I like the football-shaped glasses with slushy drinks; get a combination of the Jungle Juice and Pina Colada flavors or a Banana Bayou and Brainfreeze combination for a delicious concoction! If Krispy Kreme and slushy drinks aren't unhealthy enough for you, stop by Mermaids for county-fair-style delicacies like fried Twinkies, fried Oreos, corn dogs and the relatively healthy chocolate-dipped bananas. Spandex-and-ruffle-clad showgirl types will lure you into either casino, passing out festive Mardi Gras beads.

A must-see casino for the history buff is the Golden Gate on the corner of Fremont and Main streets. The Golden Gate was the first hotel in Las Vegas, and the original building still stands. It was known as the Nevada Hotel when it opened in 1906, and a casino was added in 1955, when the property was known as the Sal Sagev (that's Las Vegas backwards, folks). Roam through the turn-of-the-20th-century San Francisco-themed casino and shuffle past the old photos of 1900s San Francisco near the check-in desk in the back. My favorite photo – which is on the wall behind the desk – shows the building the year it opened. The owner's wife

The Golden Gate was the first hotel in Las Vegas, and the original building still stands.

proudly stands in a second story doorway, looking ready to jump, but I am told she was simply waiting for some freight to be delivered. Hotel artifacts are on display throughout the casino, including vintage slot machines and a telephone from the early 1900s — back when the hotel's phone number was 1, the first in Las Vegas. That was a recurring numeral for the Hotel Nevada, whose address is 1 Fremont Street, and where rooms once were priced at $1.

Staking claim on another Las Vegas first, the Golden Gate also is home to the original bargain shrimp cocktail (which would become a Sin City staple), although inflation has brought the price up to $1.99. It's known as the "Best Tail in Town," and locals

still regularly vote it the best in the city. An estimated thirty million shrimp cocktails have been sold at the Golden Gate over the years!

From the outside of the building, facing Fremont Street, one can see a display of life-sized photos of people staring back at the street. Called "Glamorous Gamers of the Past," the pictures represent historical figures who stayed at the hotel over the years.

One of my favorite downtown restaurants is **Firefly** at the Plaza. It's the second location of this local favorite, the original of which is on Paradise Road just off the Strip. Looking a bit like a UFO hovering over the Plaza's entrance, the glass-dome-encased restaurant offers a fantastic view of the Fremont Street Experience and Glitter Gulch, plus a reinvented-retro atmosphere you may recognize from the movies *Casino* and *Get Him to the Greek*. Though Firefly is known for its tapas, it doesn't officially call itself a tapas bar anymore. Think about it: Say "tapas bar" fast and think Las Vegas. Everyone thought they were saying "topless bar," so Firefly Kitchen and Bar it is

(Left) Firefly at the Plaza, overlooking the Fremont Street Experience.

officially. The tapas are plentiful and delicious, and though I can't claim to have tried them all, the mac 'n cheese, artichoke toasts, Serrano ham and Manchego cheese, and stuffed peppers rank among my favorites. Firefly also makes some of my favorite salads in the city, so if you feel the need to stick to a diet, this could be a good spot for you.

Next to the Plaza are a couple of antique luxury train cars that lead to Main Street Station, a casino-hotel notable for its display of artwork and artifacts showcased throughout the property. They create a museum-type experience if you want to grab a brochure from the check-in counter as a guide to all of the antiques displayed and built into the establishment.

Bar Crawl

Adjacent to Main Street Station is Sam Boyd's California, which you will notice is actually Hawaiian-themed inside.

If you are looking for a few drinks and a fun night out but the typical club scene isn't for you, definitely try the bars downtown. Unique gems dot the streets, where a good drink can be found in a variety of cozy, unique atmospheres. Just east of the Fremont Street Experience is local favorite **The Griffin**. Serving stiff drinks and beer on tap, the dimly lighted, rock-music-playing establishment feels worlds away from the Fremont Street you just left. The interior resembles a medieval English pub, with beamed ceilings and fireplaces. The Griffin is at 511 Fremont Street and is open 5 p.m. to 3 a.m. daily except Sundays, when it opens at 9 p.m.

A few doors down from The Griffin, **Beauty Bar** has a completely different look but a similar best-kept-secret vibe that comes few and far between in Las Vegas. Set up to look like a 1950s beauty shop straight out of a Doris Day/Rock Hudson movie, Beauty Bar not only provides great drinks but also live music, karaoke — and manicures as well. Manicurists are on hand (no pun intended) every Friday for Manicures and Martinis, so one can have a drink and get beautified among the decor, some of which was salvaged from a salon in Trenton, New Jersey.

Right next door to Beauty Bar is **Don't Tell Mama**, an offshoot of the original New York piano bar by the same name. It's open Tuesdays through Sundays, and the singing wait staff may just inspire you to take the open mike if you've had a few too many.

Frankie's Tiki Room

Here are four reasons why **Frankie's Tiki Room** could be the best bar in town: 1. The decor is thoroughly Polynesian kitsch, done much better than at any Trader Vic's, and complete with lights made out of blowfish. 2. It's open 24 hours a day, as any self-respecting Vegas bar should be (but most aren't). 3. The drinks are tasty and the menu rates each drink with a skull count. Have a five-skull Zombie if you are looking for a good time; stick with a two-skull Pikake if you are a lightweight like me. 4. The souvenir ceramic mugs are custom-created for Frankie's and are so adorable and funny you will want to collect them all. If you want to know what I mean by funny, order the Bearded Clam. Frankie's Tiki Room is just west of downtown at 1712 West Charleston Boulevard.

Neon Museum

On Las Vegas Boulevard North, just north of downtown, is the **Neon Museum**, a surreal-looking dirt lot scattered with relics from Vegas' neon past. Some of the signs already have been restored; blocks from the **Fremont Street Experience**, the iconic Silver Slipper shoe shines above the boulevard's median, across from the mid-century conch-shell-shaped building that used to be the

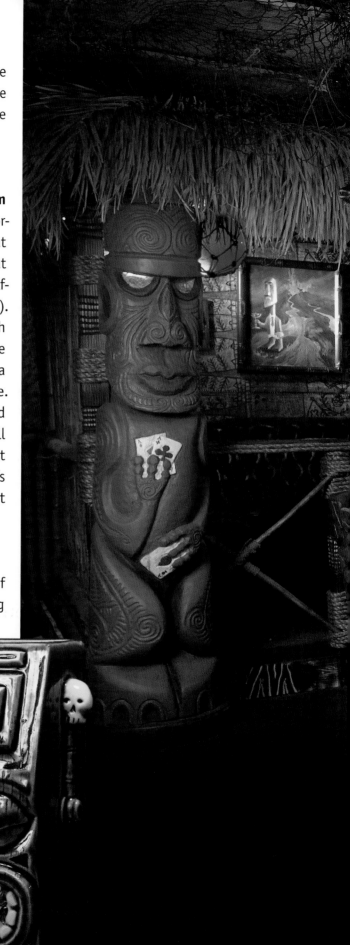

lobby of the La Concha Hotel on the Strip.

Where have these items gone? Not to die, but to live again. The Neon Museum currently is accessible by appointment only but soon will be open to the public, with the La Concha building as its lobby. (If you would like to see more of the Neon archives than just a drive-by on your trip, contact and appointment information can be found at www. neonmuseum.org.)

The humongous, whimsical structures strewn about the dusty desert lot made for a perfectly eerie, surreal and fun setting where I was fortunate enough to do a photo shoot last year. The three-acre boneyard is home to many historic pieces of signage, from the Golden Nugget's large Fremont Street sign to the Stardust's record-setting neon, the Treasure Island skull (which was replaced by, in my opinion, the much less interesting T.I. sign in 2004) and many more. The collection of more than 150 signs also includes fun, vintage fast-food signage and quirky pieces like the Coin Castle king (he looks a bit like King Friday from Mr. Rogers' Neighborhood), which used to preside over the Coin Castle Casino on Fremont Street, now La Bayou.

More of the restored signs

have been erected in and around the Fremont Street Experience.

If you are a fan of these kitschy old signs, you may enjoy driving southeast on Fremont Street, starting at Fourth Street near Neonopolis and continuing to where Fremont intersects with Charleston Boulevard. Along

the way you will see several cute '50s-era motel signs and finally, the fantastic Blue Angel weathervane at the Blue Angel motel. It was designed by Betty Willis, who also designed the iconic "Welcome To Fabulous Las Vegas" sign and the Moulin Rouge sign, among many others.

Luv-it Custard

A fabulous vintage Las Vegas treasure can be found on Oakey Boulevard just east of Las Vegas Boulevard South and a few blocks south of downtown. A refreshing departure from the Dairy Queens of the world, Luv-It Frozen Custard is a local favorite, a cute retro mom-and-pop custard stand recently featured on the *Craig Kilborn Show*. Since 1973, the walk-up-window-service establishment has survived in demolition-happy Las Vegas by providing a variety of delicious flavors of frozen custard (which differs from ice cream in that it is made with an egg base, melts slower, and has a thicker, creamier texture) on a menu that changes daily. I have yet to try all of the flavors, but so far raspberry is my favorite, and I hear a lot of buzz about the butter-pecan. From root beer floats to sundaes, the treats abound. Some people love the custard so much, they walk away with pints, quarts or even half-gallons. Luv-It is at 505 East Oakey Boulevard and is open from 1 to 11 p.m. Fridays and Saturdays, 1 to 10 p.m. the rest of the week, and is a cash-only business.

Gold and Silver Pawn Shop

Fans of the TV show *Pawn Stars* can visit the Gold and Silver Pawn Shop, open 24 hours a day, seven days a week, at 713 Las Vegas Boulevard South. Parking can be found on the streets around the shop, and although a line sometimes extends outside the doors, it usually moves pretty fast. The lovable stars of *Pawn Stars* may or may not be working in the shop at any given time, but it is fun to peruse some of the random stuff they have for sale.

143

Chapter Eight

Desert
What to Pack
How to Stay

Shopping

There are so many great, centrally located stores in Las Vegas that I enjoy shopping here more than in any other city. Casino-resorts often are lined with shops so that, in the off-chance you win at the gaming tables, they stand to make some of that money back by tempting you with luxury items! High-end resorts such as Bellagio and Wynn are peppered with such luxury boutiques.

The little Rodeo Drive of Las Vegas, however, has got to be Crystals at CityCenter. With the largest Louis Vuitton boutique in the country, a Tiffany's complete with Vegas-exclusive charms for their famous bracelets, Roberto Cavalli, Prada, Cartier and more, the beautifully designed mall not only has the most luxurious in retail offerings, but the architecture and water sculptures are themselves a reason for a visit.

For more reasonably priced shopping, my favorite is the Miracle Mile Shops at Planet Hollywood, not only for its convenient location but also for clothing and accessories at some of my favorite stores, such as Urban Outfitters, BCBG, Victoria's Secret and Marciano. These are great spots for an inexpensive, tasteful dress for a night out.

The mall with the most variety would have to be the Fashion Show Mall on the Strip, right across from the Wynn. The Fashion

Beauty:
Wear, and Refreshed

Show has six department stores (Neiman Marcus, Saks, Bloomingdale's Home, Dillard's, Macy's, and Nordstrom) and a lot of inexpensive favorites such as Forever 21 (the world's largest), and Hot Topic. Neiman Marcus and Saks are probably my favorite places to find red-carpet dresses.

My favorite places to shop for shoes are The Shoppes at The Palazzo, because they have a Barney's and a Christian Louboutin, and the Miracle Mile Shops, for more affordable options from Two Lips, Wild Pair and Bebe.

The most scenic malls are at Caesars Palace and the Venetian. They are fun to stroll through even if you don't plan to buy anything! The Forum Shops at Caesars has cobblestone floors, a faux-painted ceiling and fountains everywhere, creating a mini, air-conditioned Rome. Statues on some of the

fountains "come to life" and a 50,000-gallon salt-water aquarium adds to the eye-candy factor of this striking shopping center.

The Grand Canal Shoppes at the Venetian also are not to be missed, with canals and gondola rides weaving throughout the shopping center built around an enclosed St. Mark's Square, with painted-sky ceiling, roaming living statues, and Venetian performers. Restaurants, cafes and gelato stands complete the atmosphere of a clean, scented, mini-Venice in the middle of the Strip.

For those who like outlet shopping, I can recommend two centers — the Las Vegas Outlet Center and the Las Vegas

different reasons. The one I frequent most is the Mandara Spa at Planet Hollywood, whose Balinese-inspired treatments are the perfect way to melt away stress! I like the Mandara Hot Stone Massage and the Elimis Skin-Specific Facial, where you customize your facial to your needs. This aromatherapy facial can help dry, dehydrated skin (I recommend this for almost anyone, as the Vegas desert will quickly dry the skin), combination skin or dull skin.

My favorite pedicure in town is Mandara's Fire and Ice Pedicure, which uses a combination of cooling gels and hot stone massage as part of a sixty-minute procedure. It's the most relaxing way to fix my feet, which are always wrecked after dancing in heels six nights a week!

Speaking of my six-night-a-week gig: If you, too, were strutting the stage in next to nothing almost every night, you'd be looking out for cellulite! That's why I love the Ionithermie Cellulite Reduction Treatment when I have time. The body-contouring solution helps detoxify, speed metabolism, reduce fluid retention and tone muscles. What's not to like?

A spa definitely worth taking a look at is the one at Encore, which I think is the most beautiful in town. Photos don't really do it justice. The lobby is relaxing and breathtaking and the lockers covered in a

The gondola rides at the Venetian's Grand Canal Shoppes.

Premium Outlets at 7400 Las Vegas Boulevard South and 875 South Grand Central Parkway, respectively. The Outlet Center has a Coach, Nike, Tommy Hilfiger, Calvin Klein, and Ann Taylor Factory Store, among others. Premium Outlets has Dolce and Gabbana, Juicy Couture, Ferragamo, Lacoste, Burberry, and more.

Spas

Most every resort in Vegas has a spa. There is such a huge variety in town that I now have many favorites, for crocodile-type material that puts any designer bag to shame. The curtains are tied back with beautiful seashells and the walkway to the treatment rooms is exquisite and tranquilly lit, inviting you to come back and relax. I love the Fusion massage. I also recommend the hand-and-foot paraffin bath, which includes pressure-point massage and will moisturize and rejuvenate your hands and feet after a long day of trekking the Strip in the dry desert heat.

If you are looking for a low-key getaway, Drift Spa at Palms Place tops my list as the most chill. On the sixth floor, Drift is an oasis on the party properly, nestled next to a gym, Primo salon, and Simon Restaurant and Lounge. If I'm in the mood to hide out I love to go to Drift, get my hair done at Primp afterward and order some baked California rolls from Simon to go. The small size of Primp gives it a private, boutique-hideaway feeling that is infinitely relaxing. I love a relaxing massage and the oxygen facial is my favorite facial, leaving my skin hydrated and refreshed.

Qua Baths and Spa at Caesars Palace has several unique features worth checking out. Foremost is the Arctic Ice Room, most likely the only place you will see snow during your trip to Vegas. The beautiful blue-glass-tiled room has heated floors and benches, but the rest of the room is kept at a chilly 55 degrees while snow falls from the ceiling, making for an amazing experience unlike any other. In keeping with the resort's Roman theme, you will find a large room of three pools kept at varying temperatures, reminiscent of the

(Above) Artic Ice Room at Qua Baths and Spa, Caesars Palace. (Left) Drift Spa, Palms Place.

Roman baths of old. A large variety of services is available in addition to the usual massage and facial fare, such as Chakra Balancing, Dream Interpretation, Swarovski Crystal Body Art, Hydrotherapy, Hypnosis, Vichy showers, and more.

(Top) Mandarin Oriental Signature Spa, massage and (top right) steam room. (Right) Amp Salon, Palms.

The Spa at Mandarin Oriental is truly exquisite. In a CityCenter high-rise, it has floor-to-ceiling windows, making for gorgeous eighth-floor views of the Strip while relaxing in the Laconium Room, with heated benches and temperature-controlled chairs. I could easily spend a day relaxing and napping in the Mandarin Spa, just staring out the windows at the people on the Strip. The spa is decorated in Art Deco Shanghai-style, the robes are black and silky, and you are given a miniature cosmetics bag with toiletries upon arrival. The luxe atmosphere is topped by my favorite massage, the Mandarin Oriental Signature Spa Therapies. It starts with a consultation with a therapist, reviewing your overall health. The treatment and oils are then customized to meet your individual needs and help balance your body. The treatments were developed in consultation with aromatherapists and traditional Chinese-medicine specialists. Among the varied spa services are some Vegas-specific therapies, such as the Luminescence Massage and Body Treatment, which is perfect in preparation for a night out, and Lucky Eights, a treatment to aid recovery from long, late nights. A jet-lag therapy also is offered for the weary traveler.

Salons

Many major resorts have their own salons for the guests' convenience. Who doesn't need a good blowout the day after a wild pool party? I usually have a hairdresser come to my house for convenience, but when I do go to a salon, my favorite is Amp Salon at the Palms, where I have been going for five years. It's upscale, low-key, and a great place to get a good blowout.

What to Pack

Bathing suits: If you forget, you can always buy one in Vegas, of course. My favorite spots for swimwear are Love Jones in the Hard Rock, Molly Brown's at the Cosmopolitan, and the little boutique in the lobby of Palms Place. The Encore also has a swimwear store conveniently located across from their pool area. More resorts should do this.

Comfortable shoes: You will know what I'm talking about after a night out in your stripper heels.

Comfortable clothes: Worry about looking cute for dinner and clubbing. During the day you will be running around acting a fool, and most likely sweating your butt off. Do take note, though, that if you are here during the months of December through February, it can get quite cold. The fact that Vegas is in the desert just means it doesn't rain much; it doesn't necessarily mean it's hot year-round. But in the months of June through September, it gets REALLY hot, so beware. Even then, though, you may find yourself a little cold in some of the restaurants and shows, as they like to crank up the air conditioning, so bringing an evening wrap or jacket is never a bad idea.

A camera: Pictures on camera phones aren't that

(Right) Clockwise from top left: You can't go wrong with a simple little black dress. Add color with your shoes and accessories. ~ Surprise everyone by wearing something vintage and sexy! ~ Wear something funkier than you'd wear at home; I love this crazy feather skirt. ~ I love sparkly, glamorous, retro look, a la Sharon Stone's character in *Casino*.

great, and you don't want to accidentally text your most debauched pictures to all of your acquaintances and co-workers. Just make sure you know how to use it first. I see how tourists operate every day of the year and it seems like no one knows how to use their cameras or camera phones anymore.

Your hangover cure of choice: You don't want to go around looking for a place to buy it on the day you are actually hung over.

Travel-sized moisturizer and lip balm: Chances are it is MUCH drier in Vegas than wherever you are from. I am used to it now, but I used to always feel gross and crusty when I arrived on a trip from Southern California. My SoCal friends are always complaining of chapped lips and dry skin when they come to visit, so make sure you have a remedy on hand for the first chance you have to apply it. My products of choice are Rosebud Salve lip balm and Body Butter from the Body Shoppe. Also, bring hand cream and eye drops.

Don't overdo the body bronzer like I did in this photo. My legs look like they belong to someone else!

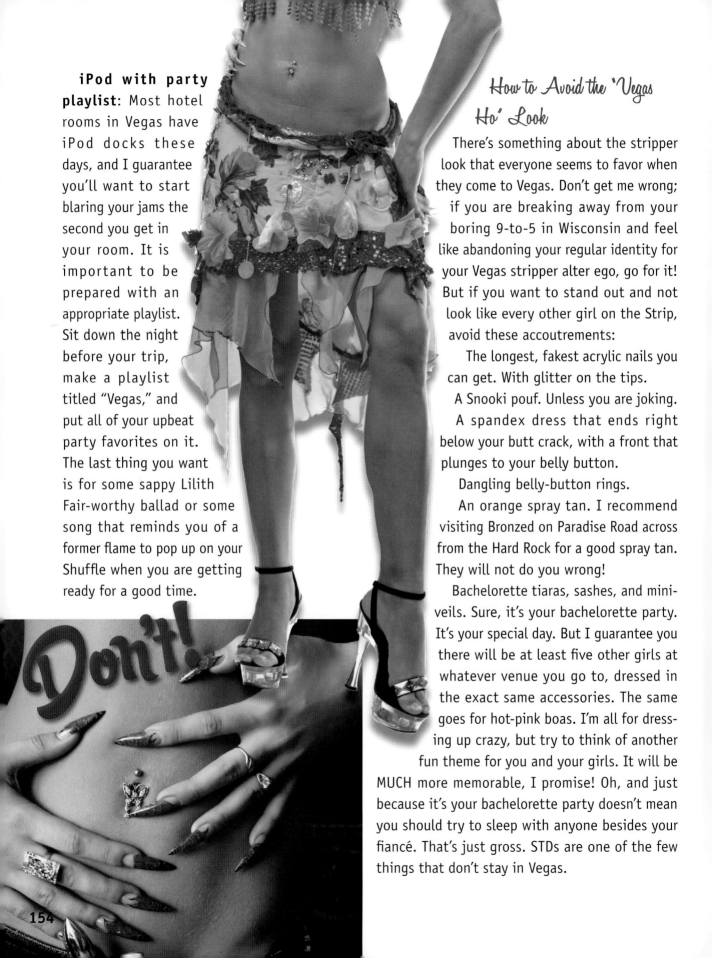

iPod with party playlist: Most hotel rooms in Vegas have iPod docks these days, and I guarantee you'll want to start blaring your jams the second you get in your room. It is important to be prepared with an appropriate playlist. Sit down the night before your trip, make a playlist titled "Vegas," and put all of your upbeat party favorites on it. The last thing you want is for some sappy Lilith Fair-worthy ballad or some song that reminds you of a former flame to pop up on your Shuffle when you are getting ready for a good time.

How to Avoid the "Vegas Ho" Look

There's something about the stripper look that everyone seems to favor when they come to Vegas. Don't get me wrong; if you are breaking away from your boring 9-to-5 in Wisconsin and feel like abandoning your regular identity for your Vegas stripper alter ego, go for it! But if you want to stand out and not look like every other girl on the Strip, avoid these accoutrements:

The longest, fakest acrylic nails you can get. With glitter on the tips.

A Snooki pouf. Unless you are joking.

A spandex dress that ends right below your butt crack, with a front that plunges to your belly button.

Dangling belly-button rings.

An orange spray tan. I recommend visiting Bronzed on Paradise Road across from the Hard Rock for a good spray tan. They will not do you wrong!

Bachelorette tiaras, sashes, and mini-veils. Sure, it's your bachelorette party. It's your special day. But I guarantee you there will be at least five other girls at whatever venue you go to, dressed in the exact same accessories. The same goes for hot-pink boas. I'm all for dressing up crazy, but try to think of another fun theme for you and your girls. It will be MUCH more memorable, I promise! Oh, and just because it's your bachelorette party doesn't mean you should try to sleep with anyone besides your fiancé. That's just gross. STDs are one of the few things that don't stay in Vegas.

154

Fun: Vegas.

Pool Parties

Over the past ten years, pools have become the way to party in Las Vegas (at least in the summer). Most resorts have them now, but a few stand out from the crowd.

Rehab at the Hard Rock: This is the original pool party, held on Sundays. I like the Hard Rock pool because it has so many features, as opposed to being just another cement pond. It has swim-up gaming, a lazy river, sandy beaches and even a little waterslide. If you are choosing Rehab as your party pool destination, get ready for crazy! It gets packed here, and this pool party has the reputation as the most debauched.

Wet Republic at MGM Grand: Locals call this one mini-Rehab. It's a popular, young pool party, but not quite as packed or as crazy as Rehab. The private cabanas are amazing, with their own private saltwater pools. The food is delicious; I love the chicken strips, waffle fries, chopped salad, mochi on a stick and push-pops.

Tao Beach: This is a slightly smaller area than Wet or Rehab, but it's a very cool see-and-be-seen spot. The menu has great Asian options like sushi and the music is always good.

Style

Chapter Nine

Ditch Fridays: I love the laid-back, young party vibe of the Palms. The pool has several fun features, like shallow areas to sunbathe or dip your feet in, a waterfall you can stand under when you need cooling off, and a glass-bottom pool above the bar for the voyeurs in the house. Ditch Friday also has my favorite yard glasses, shaped like a woman's body with a bikini and a jewel in the belly button. Try the blended Sex on the Beach!

Encore Beach Club: This newest addition to the Vegas pool party scene has parties on Sundays, Mondays, and Thursdays. The pool has a gaming pavilion and is adjacent to Switch restaurant and Surrender nightclub, for a combination of some of the best things Vegas has to offer. Shower poles for dancing and private bathrooms in the cabanas are among the great amenities.

Nightclubs

Everyone asks me which nightclubs are good on what nights in Vegas. But it's not really like L.A. or other cities, where a particular club is only good on one night.

I know Tao is especially good on Thursdays and Moon is especially good on Tuesdays, but that's probably only because I know the people who run them and they fill me in on these things. I really like XS at Encore on summer Sundays because you can jump in the pool there.

It seems there's going to be a good time at pretty much any club in Vegas. The clubs usually start to fill up around midnight or so. My advice is to pick up a *Las Vegas CityLife* (they are free and you can find them at places like coffee shops) and look at the listings in the back that tell you which nights each club is open as well as where they are located.

Tattoos

The best place to get a tattoo is Hart & Huntington Tattoo Company at the Hard Rock. Along with hasty marriages, getting a tattoo remains one of a Las Vegas tourist's most popular milestone moments.

Wedding Chapels

Las Vegas is home to more wedding chapels than anywhere else in the world. Vegas weddings have been popular since the 1930s, because Nevada marriage laws were so relaxed. Unlike in other states, there was and is no waiting period, and no blood tests are required to get a marriage license. Even as many other states have relaxed their marriage laws, Las Vegas has the reputation as the place to have an exciting, quick, inexpensive, hassle-free wedding.

Today, a marriage license costs $55 cash. All you have to do to get one is go to the Regional Justice Center at Clark and Third Streets downtown, present a driver's license or passport and fill out one easy form. The center is open from 8 a.m. to midnight seven days a week. On an episode of *The Girls Next Door*, Bridget and I tried to get a marriage license and were denied, so unfortunately same-sex marriages aren't happening right now.

If you are looking for a quirky Vegas wedding, here are a few notable chapels:

The Little Church of the West Wedding Chapel: Perhaps the most popular chapel in Vegas — not just for tourists, but for locals, too — is this historic spot on Las Vegas Boulevard South, across from Mandalay Bay. The Old-West-style chapel once was part of The Last Frontier, the second resort on the Strip. When the resort was demolished, the chapel was saved in a rare instance of Vegas conservation. Angelina Jolie and Billy Bob Thornton were wed there, both wearing blue jeans, in 2000.

Wee Kirk 'O The Heather: This is the oldest wedding chapel in Las Vegas and is at 231 Las Vegas Boulevard South, just north of the Strip. This quaint little chapel opened in 1940 and also offers Elvis wedding ceremonies.

The Artisan: There is a truly unique little wedding chapel inside this hotel. It's decorated to look like a gothic church, and the intimacy and attention to detail are stunning. Also, the Tuscany Wedding Garden behind the hotel is a beautiful shaded garden area where you can feel surrounded by tranquility just blocks from the Strip.

The Little White Chapel: Arguably the most famous chapel in Las Vegas, this one is known for the fact that Michael Jordan got hitched there and for their drive-through wedding service. It's not just pure novelty; according to the chapel's website, the owner noticed a disabled couple having difficulty getting out of their car on their way to get married at the chapel. That was the moment inspiration struck, and the drive-through service was born.

Plenty of Elvis-themed wedding packages are available at chapels all over Vegas. For the complete experience you can select a chapel that specializes in Elvis. My friend Stacey got married on *The Girls Next Door* at A Elvis Chapel at 727 South Ninth Street downtown, complete with a gold-jacketed Elvis impersonator. For an even more deluxe Elvis wedding, check out The Elvis Wedding Chapel at 1205 Las Vegas Boulevard South. Not only are there several options for an Elvis-themed wedding (Blue Hawaii, Rockabilly and Pink Cadillac, among others), but also you can book a room for your honeymoon at the E and P (Elvis and Priscilla) Suite at the same place.

Strip Clubs

Cheetah's: This is where Elizabeth Berkley's character got her start in the movie *Showgirls*. 2112 Western Avenue; open 24 hours.

The Spearmint Rhino: The Rhino is described by many as "more like a bar than a strip club," whatever that means! I know this place is super-popular, and I've seen it in the movie *Get Him to the Greek*. It must be fun, because one of my best guy friends often ends up there 'til the wee hours. And he's gay, so there must be something fun about that place besides the girls! 3344 Highland Drive; open 24 hours.

Sapphire: This one is notable because it is the world's largest strip club. 3025 South Industrial Road; open 24 hours.

Club Paradise: This gentleman's club across from the Hard Rock Hotel has a reputation as the most upscale strip club in town, with the prettiest girls. 4416 Paradise Road; open at 5 p.m. on weekdays, 6 p.m. on weekends.

Treasures: This one is known as the world's most expensive strip club and features a two-story stage and gourmet kitchen. 2801 Westwood Drive; open at 4 p.m.

My Favorite Bar

Brought to you by the owner of Frankie's Tiki Room is the Double Down Saloon, the motto of which is "You Puke, You Clean." A few blocks south of the Hard Rock at 4640 Paradise Road, the punk-style bar offers cover-charge-free music nightly, is open 24 hours and makes such locally famous drinks as the Bacon Martini.

My Favorite Drinks

I usually just drink vodka and water with ice and lemon (I call this low-calorie concoction a Skinny Bitch), but when I'm feeling like a treat, I grab one of these tasty cocktails:

Coconut Margarita from Garduno's at The Palms.

Sex on the Beach at Ditch Fridays at The Palms.

Ass Juice at The Double Down Saloon on Paradise Road.

Cheesecake shots at the Extra Lounge in Planet Hollywood Hotel.

Witch's Brew at VooDoo Steak & Lounge.

Miami Vice, a blend of strawberry daiquiri and pina colada. These are available almost anywhere they sell blended drinks.

Any cocktail at the lounge in the Mandarin Hotel. This is the best place to meet for a business drink.

Gay Nightlife

My roommate, Laura, and many of my friends, gay and straight, love Krave nightclub on Harmon Avenue, adjacent to the Miracle Mile Shops and Planet Hollywood.

Several gay bars can be found in close proximity to each other near the intersection of Paradise Road and Naples Drive, just east of the Strip and south of the Hard Rock — an area affectionately known as "The Fruit Loop." Bars with names like Gipsy, Buffalo, Piranha, FreeZone, and 8½ are all within walking distance, convenient for a fun night of bar-hopping.

Fun Stuff on the Strip

The **Mirage volcano:** This is a sight to see. Anyone can see it from the Strip, and it goes off every hour on the hour between dusk and 11 p.m.

Fountains of Bellagio: The famous fountains in front of the Bellagio play every thirty minutes during the day and every fifteen minutes in the evening, with huge fountains of water dancing to light and music.

The Sirens of T.I.: This is a free show that anyone on the Strip can see in front of Treasure Island. The show features sexy dancers, pirates, fireworks, and a sinking pirate ship and lasts eighteen minutes.

Venetian gondolas: Take a scenic ride through the Venetian or outdoors around its facade in one of the gondolas, complete with singing gondoliers! It's a mellow, relaxing ride. Tickets are sold same-day and rides are available from 10 a.m. to 11 p.m. every day but Fridays and Saturdays, when they are available from 10 a.m. to midnight.

Madame Tussaud's Wax Museum: This large collection of wax figures at the Venetian is not only interesting and fun, but a long air-conditioned stroll that is welcome after a long day in the Vegas heat. You can observe

SO MUCH M∙m∙RE THAN CANDY

My Favorite Vegas Movies

Ocean's Eleven
(the original)

Viva Las Vegas!

Casino

Showgirls

Fear and Loathing
In Las Vegas

The Hangover

— and even interact with — figures of celebrity entertainers, sports stars, historic figures and Vegas icons. It's open every day starting at 10 a.m.

M&M's World: Right next to the world's largest Coca-Cola bottle on the Strip (near the MGM Grand), this is four fun stories devoted to chocolate treats. You can find any color of M&M's candy imaginable here, along with novelty M&M's items on display

POPCORN

I had wanted to guest-star in a Las Vegas show for the longest time. I guess my fascination with live performance started with my Madonna obsession as a little girl. I would always record her videos and try to learn all of her dance routines.

More recently I became a big fan of Dita Von Teese, today's most famous striptease and queen of the new burlesque. I first saw her in 2003, when I was living at the Playboy Mansion. Hef, the other girls and I saw Dita perform at the El Rey Theater in Los Angeles and she made quite the impression.

Considering she made a big impression on me, it's strange that I can't remember what routine or routines she did in that particular show. That's probably because Hef and I had become such big fans that we would make a point of going to any show in Los Angeles that Dita was performing in. She has so many great routines; some of those I remember are a fan dance, her signature martini-glass act and a bathtub routine. Anyone who has noticed Dita in the press knows she has impeccable style and taste in fashion and beauty, and those characteristics shine through in her performances. What really sets her apart from other burlesque performers is her attention to

Peepshow

detail and production values. Props are glittered and rhinestoned, the costumes are stunning and her hair and makeup are always perfect. Besides Britney Spears' naked outfit from her 2000 *MTV Video Music Awards* performance, Dita probably is what inspired my love for all things covered in Swarovski crystals.

My other falling-in-love-with-the-stage moment came when I traveled to Europe for the first time in 2006 and saw the show at The Crazy Horse in Paris. It was so beautifully done — different from anything I had seen before. I fell in love with the music, the girls and the intimate little theater. When I found out the show existed in Las Vegas as well (it was then called *La Femme*), I had to go see that one, too. Sadly, my favorite number from the Crazy Horse Paris, Lay Laser Lay, cannot be included in the Vegas production due to local restrictions on using lasers on stage, but otherwise the show is every bit as amazing as in Paris. I had had discussions with the kind people at the Crazy Horse Paris about doing a guest appearance, but due to some havoc in my personal life, I had to back out.

Fortune works in mysterious ways, however, and despite missing out on a guest-star role at the Crazy Horse, a show better suited to me came along. When I first heard about *Peepshow* opening up at Planet Hollywood, I was skeptical. So many topless shows in Vegas just aren't up to the caliber of the Crazy Horse Paris, so I assumed this show would be of similar quality. When I heard it was set to open in the 1,500-seat Chi Theater at Planet Hollywood, I thought they were crazy! Not only was *Peepshow* set to open in the spring of 2009 — at the height of the worst economic downturn in the history of Las Vegas — but burlesque

Dita Von Teese performing in Las Vegas.

174

shows never went into theaters that large in Las Vegas! A 1,500-seat theater is usually where you find a Cirque du Soleil show.

I wasn't sure what to think, but I was definitely curious, so I went to check the show out the weekend it opened in April 2009. Needless to say, all of my

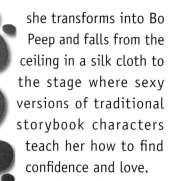

expectations were exceeded tremendously! Not only was the show exceptionally entertaining, but the caliber of talent in the cast was unbelievable. Each featured dancer seemed more talented than the last. The male lead singer had one of the most phenomenal voices I had ever heard. The sets and costumes were gorgeous and each number was charming and creative. There was singing, dancing, acrobatics and comedy all tied together with a fairy tale/nursery rhyme theme. The story line is that of a modern woman who does nothing but work, yearns for love and goes home alone to her dog at the end of the day. I felt this role suited me to a T, as that was exactly what my personal life looked like at the time. After Bo, the main character, falls asleep in the opening scene,

she transforms into Bo Peep and falls from the ceiling in a silk cloth to the stage where sexy versions of traditional storybook characters teach her how to find confidence and love.

When the show opened, Mel B. and Kelly Monaco were co-headlining. Mel B., who I was familiar with only through her work as Scary Spice in the Spice Girls, blew me away with her singing, dancing, and amazing body as Peep Diva, the lead female singer. Soap star and Playmate Kelly Monaco played Bo Peep, the role I was up for. Kelly is so petite, so in shape, and looked so great on stage that I was a little intimidated about trying out for the part. Even though I had just finished a run on *Dancing With The Stars* and had spent the past month doing the most grueling workouts of my life (six hours a day, five days a week!) I still was self-conscious. The role of Bo Peep seemed simple enough, though; she really didn't seem to do much besides descend from the silk at the beginning and dance in one feature number near the finale. I was excited. I could definitely handle this!

Still, I was really nervous when I auditioned. I wasn't that confident as a dancer and I was really shy during the topless audition because I was sure the director was going to notice every scar, bruise, half-removed tattoo and piece of cellulite on my body (at this point, I didn't realize how flattering the stage lighting in *Peepshow* is). I really wanted the role after my two auditions, but I was certainly not confident I would get it. Anytime someone auditioned or interviewed for the part, it was all over the local gossip columns. Even though I thought I was perfect for it in some ways, many of the other women who were being considered were much more high-profile than I was, and could certainly bring valuable publicity to the show.

When I finally heard that the role was mine, I was ecstatic! Even though my initial contract was only for three months (the original plan for the show was to change headliners every three months), I was determined to stay much longer. And I did. Sometimes if you work hard and believe in something, it really does happen!

As I got used to the role, I was able to become even more involved in the show and got to dance one more number. Learning from all of the amazingly talented people around me and being welcomed by everyone at *Peepshow* has truly been an amazing experience!

Peepshow is the brainchild of its director, Jerry Mitchell. Jerry is quite accomplished, to say the least. He directed *Legally Blonde the Musical*, *Love Never Dies* (the sequel to *Phantom*

WICKED WENDY

Goldie

LADY CRO

of the Opera) and *Catch Me if You Can*. One of Jerry's many other projects is *Broadway Bares*, a series of annual charity shows put on by Broadway dancers to raise money for organizations like Equity Fights AIDS and Broadway Cares. His first production of *Broadway Bares* was in 1992 and was a huge success; as the years went by, the venues required got larger and so did the amount of money raised. Starting in 1994, celebrities hosted the event, and each year performers were given a theme to develop routines around. In 1998, the theme was "Peepshow" and numbers were developed around classic storybook characters and nursery rhymes.

The *Peepshow* theme became the basis of the Las Vegas spectacular developed by Mitchell that eventually found a home at Planet Hollywood. A combination of popular and original songs coupled with Broadway-caliber talent, high production values and sexiness helped make *Peepshow* the hit it

is today. Personally, I think the combination of classic themes with grown-up yet playful sexuality mixed with a balance of contemporary and retro glamour give *Peepshow* a unique appeal not seen anywhere else in Las Vegas.

Meanwhile, Broadway Bares continues to be a powerhouse annual fundraiser. In fact, the 20th *Broadway Bares* took place this past year and we were able to put one on in Las Vegas, which was a first for the program. Josh Strickland and I hosted the event, we performed a few of the numbers from *Peepshow*, and I got to see many of Vegas' most talented dancers put on an amazing show! In total, *Broadway Bares* raised more than $1 million for charity in 2010.

Where in Las Vegas?

A.

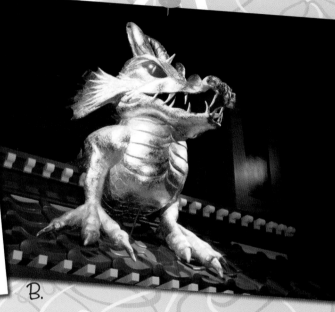

B.

C.

Answers on page 194.

D.

E.

F.

189

H.

I.

J.

K.

L.

M.

Q.

R.

Where In Las Vegas Answer Key

A. **Blue Angel Hotel** — Fremont Street and Charleston

B. **Las Vegas Hilton** — Inside

C. **The Riviera** — On The Strip

D. **Forum Shops** — At Caesars

E. **Circus Circus** — Under the porte–cochere

F. **Paris Las Vegas** — Outside

G. **Harrah's**

H. **The Miracle Mile Shops**

I. **The Sahara** — Front entrance

J. **Carpeteria sign** — 4221 W. Charleston Blvd.

K. **Planet Hollywood Casino**

L. **Le Bayou Casino** — Fremont Street

M. **Caesars Palace** — In front

N. **Excaliber** —The moat

O. **316 Fremont Street**

P. **Encore**

Q. **City Center** — In front of Aria

R. **Diamond Inn**

Photo Credits